RUNNING
FOR PEAK PERFORMANCE

FRANK SHORTER
US OLYMPIC
GOLD MEDALLIST

RUNNING

FOR PEAK PERFORMANCE

DK

CONTENTS

AUTHOR'S FOREWORD

Running changed my life forever the day I won the gold medal in the Olympic marathon in Munich, Germany in 1972. It all began, though, when I decided at the age of twelve to run to school and back several times a week because I was "training" to be a downhill ski racer. I convinced the school principal that I should wear gym shoes because I was training, even though there was a dress code that required all boys to wear regular shoes with laces to class: no casual shoes and, heaven forbid, no trainers. In gym class I was allowed to run laps around the field while the others ran relay races or played football. I must have been a very persuasive little boy.

I learned that I loved the feeling of simply moving across the ground. I could think about whatever came into my head and suddenly, I had arrived at my destination. I enjoyed the idea of being in control of the entire effort. I even modified my rubber-soled, low-cut canvas shoes to make them lighter so I could roll off the balls of my feet more fluidly as I pattered along.

I never planned on benefiting from running for the rest of my life. After all, it was just going to somehow make me a better skier. The benefits that came along with it just happened. It has always been that way with my running.

Frank Shorter

THE
BASICS

MY UNIVERSITY RUNNING COACH AND MENTOR, ROBERT GIEGENGACK, TAUGHT ME AS A FIRST YEAR STUDENT HOW TO BE MY OWN COACH. AN INTUITIVE, INTELLIGENT MAN, AND A GREAT COACH BEYOND YALE, "GIEG" ALSO HAD A BROOKLYN ACCENT AND A LISP. HE TALKED LIKE THE CARTOON CHARACTER ELMER FUDD AND ALWAYS CALLED ME "FWANKIE." DURING THOSE FIRST YEARS OF MY RUNNING EDUCATION, GIEG TAUGHT ME A LOT ABOUT MY TRAINING AND HOW IT ALL FITS TOGETHER. NOW I WANT TO PASS ON THIS UNIQUE AND PERSONAL METHOD FOR ACHIEVING YOUR RUNNING GOALS.

EFFECTS AND BENEFITS

Running is the most basic, efficient, and inexpensive way to get in shape. It can help you to lose weight, increase skeletal strength and bone mass, boost your immune system, lower your blood pressure, improve your appearance, and boost your self-confidence. The best thing about it, though, is that almost anyone can do it. We all have our own unique way of putting one foot in front of the other, and the ability to do this is all you need to start.

The training effect

Running improves your cardiovascular system through what is termed the training effect. When you exercise continuously for a period of time, your body fatigues. It then goes through the process of recovery and re-builds itself in a way that ensures that it will be just a little bit better prepared the next time. Your cardiovascular system adapts itself to these demands by strengthening your heart and actually increasing the number, size, and elasticity of your blood vessels. This increases the circulation of blood and oxygen in the body, which will most likely make your next workout at the same intensity feel easier than the last one.

Weight loss and running

Running burns more calories than almost any other exercise, so it is great way to fine-tune your weight control programme. It will boost your mood, your metabolism, and your results. Weight loss is not rocket science, but a matter of simple arithmetic: if you burn more calories, or units of energy, than you take in, you will lose weight. You must be careful about the number of calories you put into your body and use running to ensure that you use more energy than you take in (see pp80–81). Bear in mind

Lose weight: running not only makes you feel good but, if you do it regularly and in conjunction with eating a healthy diet, it will help you shed excess weight as well.

that the beginning jogger can shed weight at the same rate as the veteran runner, since you will both burn approximately 100 calories per 1.6km (1 mile), no matter what your pace. Whether you cover this distance in fifteen minutes or four, if you are training at the same level of effort (see p27), the calories used are just about equal.

Run into the future: whether you choose to run alone or with a partner, running is your investment for a lifetime of good health.

Run off your age

Running strengthens your cardiovascular system, which leads to improved circulation of blood and oxygen in the body. This increased efficiency is thought to delay the ageing process when it comes to building muscle, increasing bone density, boosting immunity, and slowing the progression of blood vessel disease. In addition to all these anti-ageing benefits, running has also been associated with promoting clearer, younger-looking skin.

For women, running offers the added benefit of staving off the effects of menopause, such as weight gain, depression, and flagging energy. It is a particularly useful weapon against a porous bone condition called osteoporosis, since the pounding of

THE RUNNER'S HIGH

The now famous "runner's high" was discovered by Dr Kenneth Cooper, the man who coined the term "aerobics" (a sustained activity, such as running, that relies on the use of oxygen for energy). One day a man came up to him and thanked him for saving his life. Dr Cooper said, "You're welcome. Would you mind telling me how?" The man had been depressed and suicidal, and since he was totally out of shape, he planned to sprint his way to cardiac arrest and get around the suicide clause in his life insurance policy. He ran a short distance from his home, collapsed, and did not die. After several attempts, running further and further each time, he realized his depression seemed to be abating. He had unwittingly discovered running as a way to cope with his depression – in other words, he had experienced the runner's high.

running actually increases bone mass. Prolonged youthfulness is not a bad side benefit from an activity that will simply make you feel better on a daily basis.

Training and mood

Along with the physical benefits, scientists are researching the psychological side of the training effect, known by many people as the "runner's high" (see box, above). After a workout, runners typically experience a surge in hormones called endorphins. These hormones are often called "happy hormones", since they elevate mood and block pain receptors in the body. The runner's high is certainly not a substitute for professional help in the clinically depressed, but it does show how effective exercise can be in lifting your spirits. On a more routine level, there is also accumulating evidence that running reduces your anxiety levels and feelings of anger.

The benefits for women: running staves off the effects of menopause by increasing bone density, preventing weight gain, and stabilizing hormones.

I believe anyone who exercises is an athlete: it is merely the level of intensity, goal-setting, and focus that differentiates one athlete from another.

THE BENEFITS OF RUNNING

A consistent running programme can change your health, appearance, and outlook on life. Here are just a few of the many perks running has to offer:

- increases fitness levels
- helps with weight loss
- improves appearance
- boosts immunity
- increases bone mass
- enhances confidence
- improves mood
- slows the signs of ageing
- stabilizes hormone fluctuations
- improves circulation
- increases energy levels
- curtails the effects of menopause
- lowers anxiety levels

HOW FIT ARE YOU?

Your heart rate is the number of beats per minute (BPM) your heart pumps blood throughout your body; it is also one of the best indicators of your cardiovascular fitness. Your resting heart rate is the key to gauging your base fitness. During exercise, your elevated heart rate can give you an accurate idea of how hard you are training, and whether you need to increase the pace, or scale it back. This section will tell you how to use your heart rate for optimum fitness.

The key to cardiovascular fitness

Let your heart rate be your guide from here on out. First, you should aim to get an idea of your resting heart rate (RHR), which is your pulse while resting. Most people have an RHR of 60–80 beats per minute, and the fitter you are, the lower your RHR will be. The time to get your most accurate RHR is first thing in the morning, before you get out of bed, and after a good night's sleep (see box, below).

Your RHR will most likely decrease as you get fitter and your heart gets stronger, but it will probably level off within the first year of training; it also tends to rise with age. However, a high RHR is not necessarily bad: world record holders have had high RHRs, even when at their best. If you have been training hard and your RHR increases, then you are probably overtraining.

BODY MASS INDEX (BMI)

BMI uses your height and weight to determine your shape's healthiness. A BMI of 18.5–24.9 is healthy, less than 18.5 is underweight, and more than 25 is overweight.

To calculate BMI in metric measurements:
weight in kilograms ÷ height in meters²
e.g. 57kg ÷ (1.7m x 1.7m) = 19.6

To calculate BMI in imperial measurements:
(weight in pounds ÷ height in inches²) x 703
e.g. (125lb ÷ [67in x 67in]) x 703 = 19.6

Maximum heart rate and training zone

Your maximum heart rate (MHR) is the fastest your heart is capable of beating in a minute. You can predict, or estimate, this figure by subtracting your age in years from 220. That said, the only time you should ever achieve your actual MHR in exercise is when you are doing a supervised, medical stress test to evaluate your cardiovascular system.

Your optimum training zone will be roughly 60–70 per cent of your MHR (see box, below left). At this rate, your body will be exercising its cardiovascular system most efficiently. It will be using oxygen to burn a carbohydrate energy source called glycogen, which is the best fuel for your training. Training at this moderate intensity will help you get fit, while avoiding the pitfalls of overtraining, such as fatigue and injury.

A word of caution

Many people run too hard during training when they don't have to. Unless you are doing the long runs (90+ minutes) or intense interval (see pp112–17) or hill training (see pp118–19) of someone wanting to race, you never need to run at a heart rate higher than 70 per cent of your MHR. This training should only be started after about a year of easy running and, even then, you should not push your heart rate above 80 per cent of your MHR. It is not sustainable for more than a few minutes and can lead to overtraining (see pp66–67).

HEART RATE FITNESS FORMULAE

Use your pulse to determine your cardiovascular health and optimum training intensity. Use the following three basic formulae to calculate your fitness level:

Resting heart rate (RHR) = first thing in the morning, count your pulse for 10 seconds on your neck just below your jaw bone, or on your wrist (*see right*). Multiply this figure by 6.

Maximum heart rate (MHR) = 220 minus your age.

Aerobic training zone (60–70 per cent of MHR) = your MHR (*see above*) × 0.6 or 0.7.

Aerobic versus anaerobic

Simply put, aerobic means with "enough oxygen". Muscle movement involves processing either glycogen (a simple sugar), or fat and protein (less efficient energy sources than glycogen) with oxygen from the air to fuel muscle contraction. At a certain level of effort (starting at 70–80 per cent of your MHR) and after a certain period of time, the body is unable to take in enough oxygen to keep up with the demands of its metabolism. The higher your heart rate is, the sooner you will hit this threshold. The muscles then process the energy source anaerobically or "without enough oxygen". This inefficient process also produces a by-product called lactic acid, which builds up in the muscle, eventually causing the muscle to cease contraction.

So if you are running at an anaerobic level, then you will be unable to sustain this state for more than about three minutes. However, you do not need to "go anaerobic" to improve cardiovascular health; aerobic training will get you fit, healthy, and strong.

Your RHR is the key to your fitness and training: check it every morning, and record the figure. This way, you can see if you are getting fitter (the number decreases), or if you have been training too hard (it goes up).

WHAT TO WEAR

Running clothes are designed to be comfortable and functional. Tried-and-true materials that stay dry, while allowing moisture to pass through to the outside air, add to the price but are definitely worth the expense. They are lighter, durable, and keep you drier and warmer than cheaper fabrics. Constantly experiment with layering your clothes in order to achieve protection from the elements without overheating.

You get what you pay for

At the high end of the clothing price range are the windproof, breathable, and waterproof fabrics worn as the outer shell. In simple terms, waterproof fabrics allow moisture in the form of water vapour to wick away from the body, but do not allow water to get in from the outside. Think of the material as having holes that are smaller than a liquid water molecule but larger than a water vapour molecule. Waterproof fabrics will not allow water to soak through to your skin, as water-repellent fabrics do. If you are prone to overheating, bear in mind that some people actually find that waterproof fabrics keep them a bit too warm!

Layering is key

Assemble your running wardrobe in breathable layers. The goal of dressing in breathable layers is to prevent the "refrigeration effect", which occurs when perspiration on the skin evaporates and cools you off. When the wind hits the damp skin or material, this process is accelerated. As you might expect, cold wind maximizes this chilling effect. Dressing in layers with clothing that allows moisture to pass through, and away from the body, keeps you warm and dry, even when the weather is not. Whatever you do, always err on the side of more layers than you think you might need. You can always take off a layer or tie your jacket around your waist if you need to.

Base layer

Next to your skin, you should always wear garments that wick moisture away from the body and absorb none. Since most of your internal organs lie in the torso, it is the upper body that requires tender loving care in the form of wearing layers. Therefore, in dry and cool to mild weather (7–10°C/45–50°F)

WHY WICKING MATERIAL?

Always choose material that has the ability to wick moisture away from the body, such as polyester/cotton, nylon/lycra, or high-tech performance fabrics such as Coolmax®, Dri-fit®, and Micropique®. These fabrics allow moisture to pass from the skin surface through a material that stays dry while moisture collects on the outside of the material from which it can evaporate. Wicking fabrics will not prevent you from sweating, but they will keep you feeling cool and dry.

COLD-WEATHER GEAR

Good-quality running clothing can make a huge difference in your running regimen. The model below is dressed to stay warm in cold weather.

WARM-WEATHER GEAR

High-tech wicking fabrics, as well as accessories such as portable water bottles, make running in hot weather more comfortable. The model below is dressed to stay cool when the weather is warm.

A warm, woollen hat should be worn in cold weather to prevent body heat from escaping through your head.

A neck warmer can be worn around your neck and pulled up over your chin for added warmth.

A running suit made of waterproof, windproof, and breathable fabric protects your body from blustery, cold weather.

Gloves, mittens, or extra-long sleeves will keep your hands warm on chilly runs.

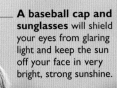

A baseball cap and sunglasses will shield your eyes from glaring light and keep the sun off your face in very bright, strong sunshine.

Wear shorts and T-shirts made of breathable, wicking fabrics to keep cool.

Always apply sunscreen to exposed skin, even if it is cloudy outside.

any long-sleeved shirt made of wicking material will keep you sufficiently warm and dry. Over that, you might wear a windproof, waterproof, and breathable running top.

For the lower body, nylon tricot shorts are fine. Though they have little wicking ability, they are durable and dry quickly. If it is windy, however, I would recommend wearing tights instead. The material of the tights is not important, but make sure the weave is dense enough to provide some protection against the wind.

Cold weather

When running in very cold weather (below 7°C/ 45°F), invest in a running suit made of waterproof, breathable, and windproof material. This may cost a little more than your typical running outfit, but the protection it provides from the elements is well worth it. For your cold-weather base layer, wear a long-sleeved shirt that wicks moisture away from the skin. In windy weather, this is particularly important, since wind on damp skin can cause hypothermia. Your middle layer should be a long-sleeved cotton shirt for wind protection. Over this, you should wear a running suit made of windproof, waterproof, and breathable material.

In cold weather, a lot of heat is lost through your head, so when in doubt, wear a hat. You can also wear a neck warmer, which can be pulled up over your chin for added warmth. Nearly all winter runners also agree that they seem to feel warmer when their wrists are covered, so make sure to wear long sleeves that you can pull down over your wrists, or wear gloves that cover the wrists as well. In the rain, wear a breathable and water-repellent or waterproof jacket over your base layer wicking garment and a pair of running tights or shorts. Wear a baseball cap or headband on your head to keep the sweat and rain off your face and out of your eyes.

SPORTS BRAS

If you are a woman, you will need to purchase a sports bra. These garments offer greater support and comfort than regular bras, since they are also designed to minimize the bouncing associated with vigorous activity, such as running. To determine whether your bra offers you enough support, perform a few jumping jacks; your breasts should remain still.

Light support

These bras are often sold in small, medium, and large sizes, rather than by cup size. They work by flattening the breasts against the body to prevent them from painful bouncing. That said, your bra should not be so tight that it constricts your breathing. If you normally wear a B-cup or smaller, a light support bra may be ideal for you.

Firm support

If you normally wear a C-cup or larger, firm support sports bras are probably your best option. They work by encapsulating each breast in a moulded cup, and unlike light support bras, they are usually sold by cup size. For optimum support, these bras should have very little vertical give in the fabric.

Front

Back

Hot weather

In hot weather (above 21°C/70°F), dress in a way that encourages sweat to collect on your skin, so it will cool you as it evaporates. You should still choose wicking garments when training in hot weather: they do not absorb much moisture, so they weigh less as you continue to sweat. Nylon tricot shorts and a vest top are the most a man would wear. A vest top can be optional for a woman wearing a sports bra (see *opposite*).

Make sure you take sensible precautions when running in direct sunlight: wear a hat, apply sunscreen (see *opposite*), and ensure you take plenty of water with you. You might also want to wear sunglasses (see *p17*) – choose ones specifically designed for running, which are designed to remain snug to your face even while moving around and sweating.

USE YOUR HEAD

In cold, blustery weather it is critical that your outer layer is made of a breathable fabric, since sweat near the skin can accumulate and cause a chilling effect to set in. If this happens, you could be on your way to hypothermia.

You should always apply sunscreen of at least SPF 15 before an outdoor run – even if it is cloudy outside. Many sunscreen manufacturers now produce sport-ready formulas: broad spectrum varieties designed to allow you to sweat freely, without running off easily or blocking your pores. Remember: all sunscreens should be reapplied regularly for full protection, even sweat-resistant varieties.

I also strongly advise wearing a hat when running in the sun to prevent overheating and dehydration. If it is very hot, however, you should take the day off, or at the very least, avoid running between 9:00 a.m. and 4:00 p.m., when the sun's rays are at their strongest.

SOCKS

Your sock is meant to fill your shoe, so the most important thing is to choose a sock that fits your foot. Ill-fitting socks will always cause discomfort and blistering, regardless of their material. There are several types of socks, but the ones listed below are three of the most common. They each have a unique selling point, but remember, their fit is key.

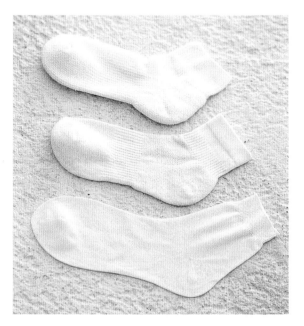

Thick cotton socks
Cotton is soft and comfortable, but when wet, it absorbs moisture and can cause blisters. This is not an ideal option if your feet sweat, or if you will be running in the rain.

Synthetic fibre with wicking capability
If you are prone to sweaty feet, or if your runs exceed 90 minutes, try socks made of synthetic wicking material.

Double layer socks
These socks prevent blisters with two layers of material, which rub against each other, rather than your foot. These are ideal for long runs and events such as a marathon.

RUNNING SHOES

There are three primary areas you should consider when buying running shoes: fit, shock absorption, and stability. In order to find your most suitable shoe, purchase your shoes from a speciality running shop where the staff has a reputation for knowledge, care, and patience. Always bear in mind that running shoes do not break in, so shopping for colour, price, or convenience rather than fit, shock absorption, and stability will only come back to haunt you (and your feet).

Finding the perfect fit

What I mean by fit is comfort. Since running shoes do not break in, the pair that feels most comfortable the first time you try them on is the pair that is best for you. All shoes are assembled around wooden moulds called lasts. The designs of these lasts can vary widely. You should be looking for a shoe made on a last that is most shaped like your foot. This is a trial and error process, and there are no shortcuts to finding your perfect shoe or size, even within the same shoe brand. Different models can be made on widely different lasts. If you cannot find a shoe that fits well enough, you may need to consider orthotics (see box, p22).

ESSENTIAL OBSERVATIONS

Your salesperson's primary concern should be your unique running needs, and these are a few of the questions they should ask you:

- how often do you run?

- what is your weekly running distance?

- do you have any pain during or after your runs?

- are you training for an event?

Your salesperson should also watch you run to see how much support you need, and whether you overpronate or supinate (see *opposite*).

TREAD WEAR

Overpronators will notice that the inside treads of their shoes wear down first. The midsoles (see p23) of their shoes are also prone to compressing and wearing out. Supinators tend to wear down the treads on the outside front of their shoes. Unfortunately, supinators also have a tendency to wear out their shoes more quickly than overpronators.

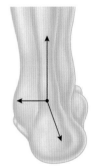

Overpronation
(left foot)

tread worn
inside

Neutral
(left foot)

tread worn
evenly

Supination
(left foot)

tread worn
outside

Shock absorption

Good shock absorption, or support, is important because your foot absorbs up to four times your body weight with each step of a run, which can be very hard on your body. This comes with a price, though, because you pay more for a midsole (see p23) made of ethyl vinyl acetate, a superior shock-absorbing material found in nearly all quality running shoes. In a pinch, you can buy shoe inserts to help absorb some of the shock, but it is better to invest in a pair of shoes with good shock absorption from the start.

Stability for overpronation and supination

You should avoid any exaggeration of the normal foot motion, called pronation. This is best described as a slight collapsing of the inside of the arch and ankle as the foot comes down in a neutral flat position and pushes off the ground while running; the foot essentially rolls inwards as it lands, or plants.

The stability of your running shoe is particularly important because it will correct any exaggerations of this foot movement. Don't worry about changing how your foot plants: just make sure the shoe you buy is designed to support or stabilize your foot's particular motion.

The two common extremes of motion are overpronation and supination (see illustration, opposite), which both describe the way the foot plants. It is the repetition of these extreme motions that causes injury. Overpronation is when the arch remains flat, and the ankle rolls too far inwards as the toes begin to push off. This increases stress on the muscles and tendons of the foot. Supination is an arching outwards of the foot before it plants, and supinators generally land on the outside of the sole. The foot then flattens into a neutral position and begins to collapse and roll outwards, or supinate. This can result in injury such as a sprained ankle.

THINGS TO CONSIDER

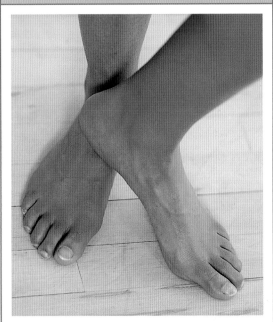

Arches: runners with painful, high arches need shoes with good shock absorption; their feet also tend to supinate. Try shoes with high arches and lots of support. Those with flat feet or low arches may overpronate, so consider a shoe designed for stability.

Different-sized feet: most people have one foot that is larger than the other. You should always buy your shoes for the bigger foot.

Changing foot size: some runners' feet actually get bigger after years of running. This may be due to collapsing arches. Accept your new size and buy accordingly.

Tread wear: your salesperson may want to see a pair of your old running shoes to determine what type of foot motion you have (see illustration, opposite). Don't panic if you don't have an old pair of shoes to hand: they can also look at your bare feet for the same information.

Wide versus narrow feet: you can purchase shoes in a variety of widths, from narrow to wide. Different brands vary in width and length, so ask your salesperson for tips to help you take advantage of the range of choices available to you.

Speciality running shops

To maximize your chances of finding your perfect running shoe, go to a running speciality shop, or at the very least, a sports speciality shop. There are running-specific shops in most major cities around the world. Search online for reviews of shops in your area, or ask other runners: the best way to find a good running shop is usually by word of mouth.

You may not know exactly which type of shoe you should be looking for, so you might be there a while. This is why your salesperson's patience and knowledge of running is key: they should not hurry you or push a particular brand on you. The person helping you with the sale should be a runner, and he or she should ask you a series of questions including how often you run and your total weekly distance (see box, p20).

Toe-striker or heel-striker?

Your footstrike should be one of the salesperson's determinations about you. Footstrike describes the way your foot lands on the ground when running. If you land on the front or ball of your foot first, then you are a toe-striker; if your heel, or the back part of your foot, makes contact with the ground first, you are a heel-striker. There is, however, no correct way to land.

In theory, you want your centre of gravity, which is located somewhere in your midsection, to be right over the point where your foot makes first contact with the ground. If you run with erect posture, you are most likely a heel-striker, and if you tend to lean forwards, you are probably a toe-striker (see pp88–89).

Since most people land heel-first when they run, running shoes evolved heel-hugging, reinforced, stabilized areas called heel counters that support the foot in this motion. These support, but do not cure, the supination and overpronation common to nearly every footstrike. If you are a toe-striker, though, heel counters are not as critical for you. Remember that comfort rules and you can feel the degree to which a shoe is supporting, or restricting, your running motion. What feels like the right balance for you generally is, because too much or too little support will be uncomfortable.

ORTHOTICS

If you can't find a comfortable shoe, you may need to see a foot specialist to determine if orthotics are necessary. Orthotics are shoe inserts (either pre-formed or moulded to the shape of your foot) that are designed to support your unique foot problems. Allow three weeks of running to adjust to them. Many people have had great success with orthotics, but they are not a panacea. If after six weeks the orthotics are still painful to wear, then they are not right for you. Discard them and schedule another visit with your foot specialist.

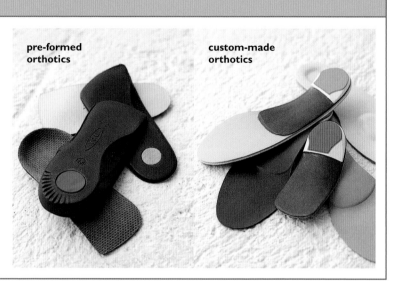

pre-formed orthotics

custom-made orthotics

ANATOMY OF A RUNNING SHOE

Get familiar with all the different parts of the
running shoe before you go shopping. This will
equip you with the knowledge to better engage
with your salesperson. It may even help you
decide which type of shoe you want and why.

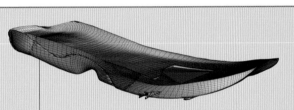

The insole
forms the inside of the shoe
and is removable. If you need
them, this is where you place
orthotics.

What does EVA stand for?
Ethyl vinyl acetate, also called EVA, is a
bunch of tiny bubbles in foam that form a
good shock-absorbing material. The bubbles
provide the cushion, but they also pop with
use. The EVA breaks down after about 4–6
months, depending on your level of activity.

The toe box
should be spacious enough
so that you have room to
wiggle your toes.

**The heel
counter**
is non-flexible
and cup-shaped
for supporting
and stabilizing
the heel. It is
particularly
important for
heel-strikers.

The midsole
provides shock
absorption and
stability. If it is a
high-quality shoe,
the midsole will
be made of EVA
(see box, above).

The upper
makes up the bulk
of the shoe and is
usually made of leather
or a lighter, breathable
synthetic material.

The outer sole
is the rubber underside of the shoe, or "treads."
It can provide shock absorption and/or durability,
depending on what type of rubber it is.

EQUIPMENT AND TECHNOLOGY

The great thing about running is that it requires so little equipment to do it. You can simply get dressed, put on your shoes, walk out your door, and run. To obtain a good idea of your training heart rate, you need only a watch and the ability to count. However, if you choose to be more precise about your training, there is a range of equipment available to help you track your progress, from basic smartphone apps to top-of-the-range fitness trackers.

Running in the digital age

For quite some time, runners typically relied on a stopwatch and some mental arithmetic in order to make a note of their progress. As technology advanced, sports shops began to stock all manner of gadgets, including GPS systems, heart-rate monitors, and pedometers, to help dedicated runners keep track of their training. Even nowadays, modern digital devices serve the same purpose: they are recording tools.

Types of technology

Modern running technology can generally be divided into one of two categories: downloadable smartphone apps and wearable fitness trackers. Each type of technology comes with its own advantages.

Running apps can be a useful way to keep a record of basic training information. They take advantage of the technology built into most smartphones, such as GPS (distance and speed) and movement sensors (step counter). Some apps can also help you plan new training routes, or show you a map of the route you have just taken. You can even input information about your body type, allowing the app to calculate the amount of calories burned during each run. With some apps available free of charge, and others costing just a few pounds, they are a great tool for beginners and casual runners.

For more advanced runners, a fitness tracker may be a more suitable piece of equipment.

CHIP TIMING DEVICES FOR RACING

When you start running races such as marathons, chances are you will hear about a device known as a chip timer or ChampionChip©. This tiny device uses special technology and bar codes to give you your exact net time and splits during your race. Some chips loop through your shoelace, while others are affixed to the back of your race number. They are waterproof and weatherproof, and work by recording your times as you run over sensor pads placed throughout the race course.

Most runners rent their chips from the race organizers, since they can only be used in races that use the matching brand of sensor pads. Chips can be picked up the day before the race, and returned after the event. You can also buy a chip from specialist running companies.

These wristwatch-like devices not only perform the same functions as a smartphone app, but are often designed to be worn 24 hours a day to encourage a healthier lifestyle. Depending on the brand and cost, fitness trackers can record the wearer's heart rate, sleep cycle, and sedentary periods, and upload the recorded information to a smartphone or computer for you to review. Top-of-the-range devices are mini computers in themselves, with the ability to play music and show you text and emails while you are out and about – features which may prove more distracting than helpful when you want to focus on your run.

Social running

Another feature, and potential benefit, of incorporating digital technology in your training programme is the potential for social encouragement. Many apps and trackers can now be linked to social media, allowing the user to share their latest run with friends, often mapping out their completed routes via GPS. Some runners find motivation in sharing this information, especially those who are looking to increase their distance or pace over time. Depending on the device, you may also be able to "compete" with friends online to see who can walk or run the greatest distance (or number of steps) during a certain period of time. These challenges and social interactions can encourage users to push themselves a little further than they otherwise might have done. While this can be great for those looking for a little extra motivation, always remember to keep your own personal goals and capabilities at the forefront of your mind. You should not overexert yourself, and risk injury, simply because you want to appear better than your friends on an app.

Choose what works for you: fitness trackers are available with a variety of different functions and extra benefits depending on how much you wish to spend.

Cost versus benefit

No matter how clever they can be, apps and trackers are by no means essential for the modern runner. Humans have been able to run perfectly well for thousands of years, and while the digital age has brought new methods of analysing our running ability, we are equally capable of recording our own training (see p70).

If you believe that an app or tracker will encourage you to run or help you record your progress, make sure to research the types of equipment available to ensure you are getting the best value for money. You may even find that a free smartphone app provides all the features that you are looking for. However much you spend (if you choose to spend anything at all), remember that no special gadget will make you a better runner overnight: genuine improvement takes time, dedication, and training.

AVOIDING DISTRACTION

No matter how many clever tricks your device can perform, do not let it steal your attention away from your training. It should be used only as an aid to your training; if you play around with it too often during a run, you will not be performing at your best.

Devices can also distract you from your surroundings. While some activities, such as listening to music, can help you relax and achieve a disassociated state (see box, p113), you should always remain aware of your personal safety:

• If listening to music, always keep the volume low enough to be able to hear traffic.

• Try not to check your phone or device too often while running, and avoid reading messages altogether, especially on uneven terrain – one misplaced step could cause injury.

GETTING STARTED

My training theory is very simple. As you begin your running programme, there are three points, which I call my rule of three, that I want you to remember for basic cardiovascular conditioning: be consistent, don't overtrain, and be aware that the duration or time of your run is more important than the distance you cover. If you can integrate these three common-sense concepts into your running regimen, then you can train yourself like an Olympian.

Consistency for flexibility

The key to success in distance running is consistency. If you consistently set out reasonable, attainable, and incremental goals for every run (see pp28–29), the precision of your effort, time, and distance will matter less and less. In other words, as you become more and more consistent with your runs, it becomes less important that you get it exactly right every time. Be very consistent and your routine will evolve naturally into the one that is best for you. This will allow you the freedom to have good days and bad days, hard runs and easy ones, without harming your fitness regimen.

The myth of overexertion

Contrary to what you might think, easy runs do play a large part in improving your fitness. There is indeed a misconception that overexertion yields maximum results. Successful coaches and runners have always known what recent research has confirmed: that most running for basic conditioning should be done at a relatively easy pace, at which you can still maintain a conversation. This is called conversational pace.

There is no requirement that you talk while running for cardiovascular fitness, but you should always have enough breath to speak with every step you take. If you cannot carry on a normal conversation while running, or if you find yourself having to stop to take a deep breath every once

in a while, you are going too fast. It is a natural tendency for us to test our limits, and this is the trap that many beginning runners fall into. They train too hard and too fast, needlessly exhaust themselves, and then write off running as impossible.

There is another, better way to train, since we all have the innate ability to pace our effort evenly and efficiently over an extended period of time. Everyone has the ability to feel what does and does not work for his or her own body. This instinct, called the rate of perceived effort (see opposite), simply needs to be sharpened. Once honed, it will tell you not to mimic the professional team athletes' short bursts of energy in your training. It is not sustainable for much more than three minutes because, unlike you, they're not training – they are competing, they are racing.

It's only a matter of time

When you begin your running regimen, bear in mind that the time you spend on your feet running is more important than the distance you cover. (Distance is a secondary concern that becomes important when you are training for a race of a specific length.) When you base your runs on time rather than distance, it makes it very difficult to overtrain or overexert yourself. Instead of charting a 1.6km (1 mile) route and running it too fast, or exhausting yourself in the first half and having to walk the second half, simply plan to run for ten minutes at a comfortable pace. In order to do this, you will need to learn how to determine how hard your heart and lungs are working as you run.

Rate of perceived effort

You may have heard of the rate of perceived effort (RPE) scale. It is the quickest and most accessible way to determine how hard your cardiovascular system is working while exercising. On a scale of one to ten, most people can accurately estimate their level of effort while exercising. One to five on this scale represents non-exercise heart rates – you can breathe easily, talk, or even sing. Eight to ten on this scale represents extreme exertion: at eight, conversation is just possible; at nine, maintaining a conversation is very difficult, and at ten, impossible. Your aim is to hover between six and seven on this scale: at six, you should slip into a slightly breathless state, but speaking is fairly easy, and at seven, breathing becomes more laboured: you can talk, but you won't want to.

If you have been completely sedentary, just take a brisk walk with a ten-minute time goal and see if at some point along the way you feel yourself slipping into a slightly out-of-breath state – this would be level six on the RPE scale, which is roughly 60 per cent of your MHR, (see pp14–15). Be willing to slow down or even stop if at any point you feel your RPE level rising above six. If you have no trouble walking the ten minutes, try walking faster, or even jogging. Your personally-determined RPE of level six will be your benchmark for improvement and for retrospective stories in the future: "believe it or not, when I started out, I could only walk this fast and for this long." As you get fitter, you'll be able to run faster and longer at your RPE level six. Once you decide what your goals are and get a feel for your unique RPE levels while exercising, getting started is easy. The great news about my training

Conversational pace: you should always be able to maintain a conversation while on training runs. If you cannot talk, then you are going too fast.

theory is that the type of aerobic activity you perform is transferable – that is, you can run, cycle, swim or use aerobic machines at the gym (at the same RPE level) to achieve the same fitness results as running. Simply select activities based on what feels most comfortable and natural. As you become a fitter and stronger runner, try supplementing your programme with some other forms of aerobic exercise. This will not only prevent boredom, but it will inhibit injury as well.

THE FIRST RUN

With running, as with anything, it takes courage to get out there and get started. The first run is always the scariest and the toughest, but you must have faith in your body and its power to adapt to this new activity. If you set yourself reasonable goals, and run consistently right from the beginning, your body will acclimatize itself and your subsequent runs will become easier and more pleasant. Then, in no time, you'll be hooked on running.

Setting goals for success

Before embarking on your first run, you must learn the most basic principle of training, regardless of age, gender, or level of ability: that is, how to set yourself running goals for success. My university running coach and mentor, Robert Giegengack, or "Gieg", as I called him, taught me that training and racing goals should always, always be reasonable, attainable, and incremental. This has been the mantra by which I have set my goals throughout my running career. By integrating his three simple concepts into every goal I've set for myself, Gieg taught me how to be my own coach, and now I'm passing this knowledge on to you.

Reasonable, attainable, and incremental goals

When setting yourself a reasonable goal for your first run, don't worry about speed or form: time is of the essence. You should simply aim to jog for as many minutes as you feel comfortable and "within yourself." Remember to go easy in the beginning, and don't be afraid to jog slowly or even walk if you need to.

Set yourself a clearly attainable goal – by attainable, I mean setting a goal that you know you can accomplish. This could be to jog for as few as five minutes at RPE level six; you can always add a little more time at the end if you are feeling strong. Remember that you are setting your benchmark for improvement. The point is to achieve your initial goal, and when possible, exceed it in small increments. These small and frequent achievements will boost your confidence and encourage you to stick with your running regimen. In increments, slowly build up the time you spend on each session, and eventually you'll be running for longer than you ever thought possible.

Goal-setting: always set yourself reasonable, attainable, and incremental goals. After all, you're setting your benchmark for improvement.

What about long-term goals?

In addition to your day-to-day, reasonable, attainable, and incremental goals, you should also have a long-term goal in the back of your mind. It could be any number of things, from losing weight to feeling better to improving fitness. Be careful, however, not to fixate on it, or let it distract you from your smaller, incremental goals. A reasonable ambition for any beginner is to be able to run for 30 minutes continuously, three times per week. It may sound hard right now, and you should take as long as you need to get to this level, but if you consistently set yourself reasonable, attainable, and incremental goals, eventually you will get there.

The two-week, two-month rule

If you are new to running, your body may feel a bit strange in the beginning, since it is not used to this movement. This is normal, and it is because your body and its muscle memory have "forgotten" how running is supposed to feel. Even Olympic runners

Think short-term for the long-term: to achieve long-term goals, such as running 30 minutes, three times a week, start with setting yourself small goals.

GOAL-SETTING POINTERS

We all have bad or weak days and good, strong days, so tailor each individual goal to how you are feeling, both psychologically and physically.

Set a clear and attainable goal right before you step outside to run. After all, you can't know how you are going to feel the next day if you set Wednesday's goal on Tuesday morning.

Be flexible, and never force yourself into a run that you are not feeling ready for. Assess the situation during the run as well, setting yourself goals in five-minute intervals.

Decide in the middle of your workout if you want to "push the envelope" or stop, adding five minutes at a time if you feel strong. Try to work up to 30 minutes of continuous running, three times per week, but take as long as you need to get to this level.

who have taken time off feel a bit awkward when they begin to run again. You must give your body time to acclimatize to this new activity, and this takes about two weeks.

This adjustment period actually involves the development of neural patterns, known as muscle memory, in the body. In essence, you are training your muscles to "remember" the movement of running. The more you run, the better-trained your muscles will be to "remember" the movement, and the more natural your body will feel while doing it.

After two months, your muscle memory will be so well adapted to running that your body will actually be ready for a new challenge. Your running will then begin to improve. This adjustment period is what I call my two-week, two-month rule: two weeks to adjust to the new activity or movement, and two months to improve, or build on it.

The benefits of group running

It is best to seek out a running group very early in your training, since training in a group can be beneficial on many levels. If you know someone who runs and he or she is a patient person, you should ask them to run with you. At the most basic level, a running group or partner provides moral and psychological support, and the team element will motivate you to show up so you won't let the group down. Running in a group also offers the added benefit of safety in numbers.

The group and conversational pace

Talking while running keeps the group rolling along at conversational pace, the optimum speed for cardiovascular conditioning. Talking also introduces you to the concept of dissociating, which is thinking about being somewhere other than where you happen to be. (*For more on dissociation, see box, p113.*) When you are running easily, it is often fun to dissociate, to imagine yourself in a different place and situation. It is very relaxing and it helps the time pass more quickly.

The ideal partner

The best running partner is someone whose ability is equal to or slightly better than your own. Running with someone of nearly equal ability helps at both a physical and emotional level, but your running partner should be patient above all else. He or she should understand that improvement takes time and that training has its ups and downs, both physical and mental. A good partner recognizes when the other is having an off period and is willing to wait for his or her friend.

Not only do you support and encourage each other when you're having a bad day, but you may even find that you can actually start to fall into each other's rhythms and help pull each other along. The trailing runner may fall into stride and be pulled along by the rhythm of the runner in front; the stronger runner serves as an incentive for the other to run faster.

Don't worry if you can't find a suitable partner immediately – running partners and running groups seem to find each other, but it does take time and a little effort. Some good places to start looking though are running speciality shops, health clubs, gyms, or community centres.

What if I'm too shy or too slow?

As a general rule, runners are very accepting of new people, so you should never feel intimidated or worry about elitism when joining a running group. Even the "uniform" of shorts, T-shirts, and running shoes is a great social equalizer. In all my years of running, I have never been able to see any correlation between someone's level of education or his or her financial or social success and the way he or she dresses to run.

It's not a race: above all else, your running partner should be patient with you. Simply put, find a patient partner, or find a new one.

Running in loops: there's no shame in stopping. Feel free to peel away when you've had enough, and the rest of the group can continue on their run.

Loops for success

We're all different, so when running with a group, aim for runs that consist of loops, rather than circular or A to B routes. Since speed is not a factor, groups will often set out to run a series of loops so that people can stop when they have reached their personal limit. I term this limit your "energy quotient," which is the point at which you simply know you have done enough exercise for that particular day. This will allow you to run at your own level, even while running with others. Simply stop when you've had enough, and your partner can continue to run. A good running group understands that training does not mean competition. Running a familiar route or loop is like reading a good book: if you let your mind get involved, the time seems to pass more quickly than it would normally. When a group goes out to run a familiar loop, rather than concentrating on navigating their route, they can let their minds and topics of conversations wander. The run seems easier and the time flies.

TECHNIQUE AND SAFETY

We've covered all the basics on getting started, from setting achievable goals to discovering your conversational pace to finding your ideal running partner(s). The following two pages offer some small, but essential, tips on how to ease safely into your new running regimen. When beginning your new running routine, use the following advice for the greatest chance of success and a minimal chance of injury.

Routes and surfaces

Many people feel that running is a meditative sport, since it allows you private time to lose yourself in thought. Because of this, you should seek a course that becomes comfortable and familiar, and preferably crosses very few streets. Repetition of a certain running loop is fine; you may even choose to run laps on your local track. This awareness of your your mind can (safely) wander from time to time. Try to vary your route in small ways to avoid injury through the constant and unceasing, day-after-day

Ideal surfaces: try to run on surfaces that absorb some of the shock of impact, such as dirt or grass, and vary your routes and surfaces occasionally to prevent injury.

repetition in the same groove. Have three runs and alternate them regularly, or occasionally switch the direction of your loop (see pp122–23). Bear in mind that most running injuries result from overuse, and pain while running is an indication that something is wrong. Ignoring the pain accelerates the injury process.

The shock of your foot striking concrete is very hard on your body, so try to plan a route that has a soft surface, such as grass, dirt, or indoor and outdoor sports tracks. These surfaces have more "give" – that is, the surfaces themselves, rather than your foot, absorb much of the shock of impact. The jarring of going up and coming down off kerbs can also cause orthopaedic, or skeletal, injury, so you should avoid them as well (see pp120–21). Regardless of your surface or route, though, the impact of running takes its toll, and the body makes you aware of this through pain. If you stop the repetition soon enough and allow time for recovery, the wearing-out will not reach a crisis point.

Technique and breathing for beginners

There is no such thing as one correct running technique. Running is an intuitive and common-sense sport: you instinctively knew how to run as a child, and you should not worry about running form now. If you experience pain or discomfort while running, it is an indication that your body does not want to move in that particular running motion.

Simply run in the manner you find most comfortable and your form will be right.

As with technique, breathing is a common-sense issue. Forget what you've read or heard: you've been breathing all your life and no one can tell you how to do it better than you already know how. However you can most effectively get oxygen into your lungs is the best way for you to breathe.

Always make time for recovery

A mistake that many runners make is to do too much, too soon. During the first two weeks, your cardiovascular system has to adjust to this new, or perhaps long-forgotten, movement and the stress it causes your body. It is therefore critical that you

Easy first run: in the beginning, your runs should be gentle and easy, with an adequate number of rest days in between. This will give your body a chance to recover thoroughly.

start slowly and build in time for recovery. This time allows your body to re-build and replenish torn-down muscles and tissue. When you start running, a good rule of thumb is to run easy and follow every day you run with one where you do not – in other words, a rest day. You will be recovering for the first time in years, maybe ever, following these initial runs. Over time, though, you will begin to recover more quickly and efficiently.

BEGINNER'S PROGRAMME

Now that you know all the basics, it's time to get started on your training. The important thing at this stage in your running, and indeed throughout your running career, is that you're making incremental improvements on your current fitness level. Always run at conversational pace, taking adequate rest days in between. At this point, base your reasonable, attainable, and incremental goals on time, not distance. The programme on the right is meant to be used as a guideline, and not an exact formula for your workouts.

Weeks 1–4 Start with short runs, setting goals that you know you can complete. Build up the length of your runs slowly, starting with whatever you find comfortable. In the first two weeks, remember the two-week, two-month rule (see p29): it will probably take two weeks for you to adjust to running.

Weeks 5–8 During this period, you should be easing into your programme. You should be more comfortable with the running motion, and you will most likely have discovered the runner's high. According to the two-week, two-month rule, after week eight (roughly two months), your body should be ready to move on to the next level.

☐ Rest days
▨ Run days

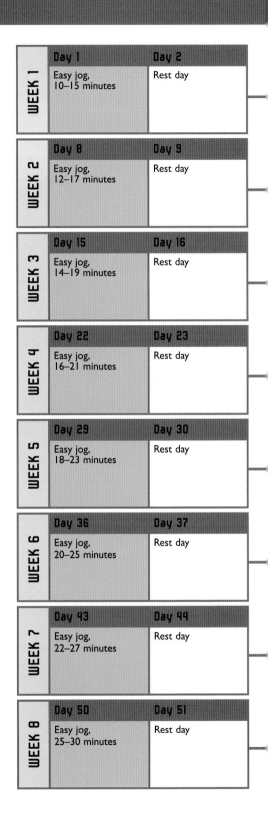

WEEK 1
Day 1	Day 2
Easy jog, 10–15 minutes	Rest day

WEEK 2
Day 8	Day 9
Easy jog, 12–17 minutes	Rest day

WEEK 3
Day 15	Day 16
Easy jog, 14–19 minutes	Rest day

WEEK 4
Day 22	Day 23
Easy jog, 16–21 minutes	Rest day

WEEK 5
Day 29	Day 30
Easy jog, 18–23 minutes	Rest day

WEEK 6
Day 36	Day 37
Easy jog, 20–25 minutes	Rest day

WEEK 7
Day 43	Day 44
Easy jog, 22–27 minutes	Rest day

WEEK 8
Day 50	Day 51
Easy jog, 25–30 minutes	Rest day

Day 3	Day 4	Day 5	Day 6	Day 7	Total
Easy jog, 10–15 minutes	Rest day	Easy jog, 10–15 minutes	Rest day	Rest day	30–45 minutes

Day 10	Day 11	Day 12	Day 13	Day 14	Total
Easy jog, 12–17 minutes	Rest day	Easy jog, 12–17 minutes	Rest day	Rest day	36–51 minutes

Day 17	Day 18	Day 19	Day 20	Day 21	Total
Easy jog, 14–19 minutes	Rest day	Easy jog, 14–19 minutes	Rest day	Rest day	42–57 minutes

Day 24	Day 25	Day 26	Day 27	Day 28	Total
Easy jog, 16–21 minutes	Rest day	Easy jog, 16–21 minutes	Rest day	Rest day	48–63 minutes

Day 31	Day 32	Day 33	Day 34	Day 35	Total
Easy jog, 18–23 minutes	Rest day	Easy jog, 18–23 minutes	Rest day	Rest day	54–69 minutes

Day 38	Day 39	Day 40	Day 41	Day 42	Total
Easy jog, 20–25 minutes	Rest day	Easy jog, 20–25 minutes	Rest day	Rest day	60–75 minutes

Day 45	Day 46	Day 47	Day 48	Day 49	Total
Easy jog, 22–27 minutes	Rest day	Easy jog, 22–27 minutes	Rest day	Rest day	66–81 minutes

Day 52	Day 53	Day 54	Day 55	Day 56	Total
Easy jog, 25–30 minutes	Rest day	Easy jog, 25–30 minutes	Rest day	Rest day	75–90 minutes

PREPARATION AND RESISTANCE TRAINING

DO NOT GIVE IN TO THE IDEA THAT YOU ARE WASTING PRECIOUS RUNNING TIME AND EFFORT BY FOLLOWING A PREPARATION AND RESISTANCE TRAINING ROUTINE. THESE ARE ELEMENTS OF COMPLETE AND BALANCED HEALTH THAT WILL HELP YOU ATTAIN OPTIMUM RUNNING PERFORMANCE. IT SHOULDN'T BE PAINFUL EITHER: IT SHOULD NEVER HURT WHEN YOU STRETCH AND DON'T STRETCH ANYTHING IF IT HURTS.

WARMING UP

Anyone who has ever felt stiff when getting out of bed in the morning can appreciate the need to warm up at the beginning of a workout. Abrupt increased demands on your body can often have unpleasant consequences, such as stiffness, cramps, and even injury. Warming up before a workout slowly acclimatizes your body to the stress of vigorous exercise by increasing blood flow to your working muscles – literally warming them up, and making them more supple.

My warm-up

Cold, stiff muscles are more vulnerable to strains and injury, so warming up is an essential part of any exercise programme. It is one of the best ways to prevent injuries, so always make time for it before your workout. Never stretch before you warm up (known as static stretching): this can tear the cold muscles and cause injury. The best way to warm up and stretch your muscles for running is to walk quickly or jog very slowly, with a more restricted range of motion. Maintain this pace, gradually speeding up for five to ten minutes until you hit your training pace. This is known as active stretching, where the muscles are warmed up for an action by going through the motions for that action slowly and gently. This is an area where common sense and physiology go hand in hand: you can never warm up too slowly, so do what feels most natural for you.

Your warm-up pace should be 20 per cent slower than that of your conversational pace. In other words,

Always static stretch after your workout, and never before. If you feel you must stretch before your training run, do so only after a five-to-ten-minute warm-up jog. In my view, static stretching helps prevent injuries, not cure them. When in doubt, you should take a break from this kind of stretching.

it should be level five of your RPE (see p27), which corresponds to very, very light exertion. This can also be expressed as 40 per cent of your MHR (for formula, see box). You should be just barely slipping into a slightly breathless state. This slow version of your workout is the most natural and least jarring way to stretch for your run.

Bear in mind that it is not your speed that is important – it is your level of effort that counts. If your warm-up walk or jog increases your blood flow, circulation, and heart rate, then you are going fast enough; when your instincts are telling you to go faster, you're doing it right.

WARM-UP FORMULA

A good formula for determining your ideal warm-up pace and exertion is 40 per cent of your MHR. To calculate this figure, see below:

Maximum heart rate (MHR) = 220 minus your age

Your warm-up heart rate and pace = MHR x 0.40

THE HUMAN BODY

Get familiar with your anatomy. Consult the annotated pictures below to learn how your muscles, tendons, and bones are interconnected.

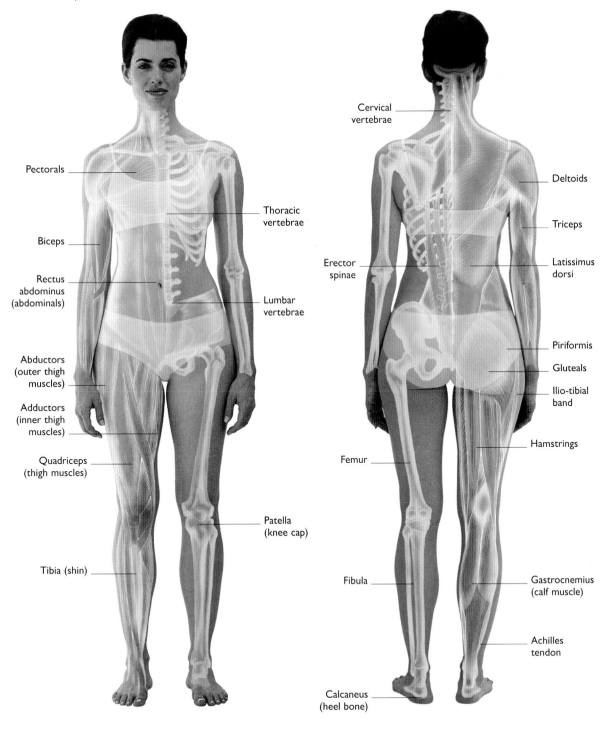

Pectorals

Biceps

Rectus abdominus (abdominals)

Abductors (outer thigh muscles)

Adductors (inner thigh muscles)

Quadriceps (thigh muscles)

Tibia (shin)

Thoracic vertebrae

Lumbar vertebrae

Patella (knee cap)

Cervical vertebrae

Erector spinae

Femur

Fibula

Calcaneus (heel bone)

Deltoids

Triceps

Latissimus dorsi

Piriformis

Gluteals

Ilio-tibial band

Hamstrings

Gastrocnemius (calf muscle)

Achilles tendon

COOLING DOWN

Cooling down is an important part of your running programme. It helps flush out lactic acid from your muscles, allows your heart rate to gradually return to its resting state, and helps restore your body to its resting equilibrium. Your cool-down can be as long as you wish, but it should never last fewer than three minutes. Whether I have just finished a training run or crossed the finish line of a gruelling race, I always jog very slowly for at least three minutes to allow my body to recover.

The beginner's cool-down

Jogging slowly or walking for three to five minutes is a sufficient cool-down for the beginning runner. It will help slowly bring your pulse back to a normal, resting level. If you have maintained your conversational pace during your run, you will not have gone anaerobic. Since you have trained within your aerobic zone, your muscles will not have accumulated lactic acid, which is a by-product of anaerobic training. Because of this, your cool-down walk or jog is not critical, but it is a good habit to get into.

Cooling down after easy runs

The above guideline also applies if you are an intermediate or advanced runner who has just completed an easy, conversational pace run. In both cases, you will have trained within your aerobic zone, and so your body will not have produced toxic by-products associated with hard anaerobic exercise. In this instance, cooling down simply allows your body to ease back into its normal state.

Cooling down after hard runs

The harder you train, the greater your need for a thorough cool-down. Hard workouts, which include long runs (90+ minutes), interval training (see pp112–17), hill training (see pp118–19), or racing all involve going anaerobic at some point, so it is absolutely critical that you cool down sufficiently by jogging slowly for at least ten minutes. Training at an anaerobic level means that your muscles will have produced lactic acid, free radicals, and other toxins, all of which can cause muscular aches.

Cooling down after hard training is essential for flushing out these exercise by-products in order to prevent muscle soreness. Failure to do so could have unpleasant consequences, ranging from strain-induced injuries to post-workout stiffness. It can also contribute to a condition known as Delayed Onset Muscle Soreness (DOMS), which is muscular pain and soreness that occurs after as many as two days following a hard workout.

Tips for cooling down

You should feel as though you are slowing down significantly, but doing so gradually is key. What feels most comfortable is probably the ideal cool-down pace for you. However, if you prefer a more concrete calculation, simply use the warm-up formula (see box, p38) to determine your cool-down starting point. From there, slowly begin to decrease your pace over the course of your cool-down. Follow your cool-down with the series of stretches on pages 42–49 in any order you wish.

Cooling down: always finish your run by jogging slowly for at least three minutes. After a hard workout or a race, jog slowly for a minimum of ten minutes.

HAMSTRING AND CALF STRETCH

Having flexible muscles and tendons in the backs of your legs is crucial for avoiding injury and running your best. The following stretch targets this area by lengthening the hamstrings, as well as the calves and the adjacent Achilles tendons. The resulting suppleness will promote a greater range of movement in the legs, which, in turn, will help you to run smoothly.

1 Sit on the floor with your legs out in front of you at a right angle to your torso. Relax your arms and press the backs of your knees into the mat.

2 Keep your back straight and your torso lifted, as you slowly bend your upper body forwards, feeling the stretch in your hamstrings in the backs of your thighs. Reach your arms forwards and grab hold of the balls of your feet, allowing your knees to bend slightly, if necessary. You should now feel the stretch not only in the hamstrings, but also in the backs of your calves. (To advance this stretch, aim to straighten your legs as you hold the balls of your feet.) Hold this position for 5–10 seconds, then relax. Repeat twice.

keep back straight

feel it here   *feel it here*

HIP, BACK, AND SIDE STRETCH

Performing this stretch is an excellent way to prevent groin strain, as well as tightness in the muscles along the sides of the body, including those in the back and hip. This stretch also helps to loosen tense abdominal muscles, which may be responsible for the "stitches" or cramps in the torso that runners sometimes get.

1 Sit on your mat in a centre-split position. Slowly bend your right leg in towards your body, keeping your left leg extended straight out to the side.

2 Twist your body to the left towards your extended leg, placing both hands as far down your calf as you can. Bring your chest and torso as close to your extended leg as possible, feeling the stretch along the right side of your hip, back, torso, and your left inner thigh. Hold this position for 5–10 seconds, then relax. Switch legs. Repeat twice on each side.

bring chest towards leg

feel it here

feel it here

HIP STRETCH I

Running may cause tightness in the hip muscles and in the piriformis, which is a muscle located deep in the buttock. When inflamed, the piriformis can put pressure on the sciatic nerve in the lower back, which may result in back pain. The most effective way to relieve this ache, and loosen the surrounding muscles, is to perform the following stretch.

hold knee here

feel it here

twist upper body

1 Sit upright with your legs straight out in front of you. Bend your right leg, bringing it across your left thigh as you sit up straight. Hold your right leg in position at the knee.

2 Hold your lower body static as you twist your upper body to the right. Place your right hand on the ground behind you for balance and your left elbow against the outside of your right knee. Press your left elbow against your right leg to maximize the stretch in the piriformis muscle. Hold this position for 5–10 seconds, then rest. Switch legs and repeat twice on each side.

HIP STRETCH II

Runners frequently overlook the importance of stretching their hips thoroughly, since the piriformis muscle can get tight without showing early symptoms. This stretch works the piriformis more deeply than hip stretch I (*see opposite*), but it should be performed in addition to, and not instead of, the first hip stretch. These stretches will prevent any shortening or tightening of the piriformis.

1 Lie flat on your back with your knees bent. Bend your right leg to the side, placing the outside of your ankle just above your left knee.

2 Place both hands behind your left thigh and pull your leg up towards your torso. Both legs should now be lifted off the ground. This multi-tasking movement will stretch your buttocks and lower back, as well as your hip. Hold this position for 5–10 seconds, then rest. Switch legs and repeat twice on each side.

pull leg towards body

feel it here

LYING QUADRICEPS STRETCH

This deep stretch targets the large muscle in the front of your upper thigh called the quadriceps. Running relies heavily on the quadriceps to propel your body forwards. It is therefore essential that you stretch this area properly to flush out any accumulated toxins in the muscle, such as lactic acid and free radicals, that may lead to soreness.

1 Lie on your left side with one leg on top of the other. Prop yourself up on your left elbow, placing your right hand flat on the ground in front of you for balance. Hold your body long and straight on the floor.

2 Bring your right leg up behind you and hold the front of your foot with your right hand. Pull your foot close to your body, holding your calf against your hamstring, pushing your right hip forwards slightly. You should feel an intense stretch in the front of your right thigh. Hold this position for 5–10 seconds, then relax. Switch sides. Repeat twice on each leg.

push top
hip forwards

feel it here

STANDING CALF STRETCH

This is an excellent stretch for both the Achilles tendon and the calf muscle, also known as the gastrocnemius, in the back of your lower leg. The calf muscle is one of the strongest muscles in the body, and runners frequently suffer from stresses and strains due to tightness in this area. This move also stretches the arch of your foot, an area that is often overlooked in stretching regimens.

2 Lean your upper body in towards the wall, placing the pressure of your weight on the ball of your right foot. Push your weight towards the wall, using your back foot to increase the stretch. Make sure you do not bounce while performing this stretch. You should feel an intense stretch in the calf of the leg that is closer to the wall. Hold this position for 5–10 seconds, then relax. Switch legs. Repeat twice on each side.

1 Stand upright, facing a wall, and roughly 30cm (12 inches) from it. Bring your right leg forwards, placing the ball of your foot against the wall.

push forwards
with back foot

feel it here

TRICEPS STRETCH

Do not overlook the importance of stretching your upper body, since many runners store tension in this area without even realizing it. If you supplement your running with resistance training, it is even more important that you stretch the muscles you are targeting. The following move is a stretch for the triceps muscle, located in the back of your upper arm.

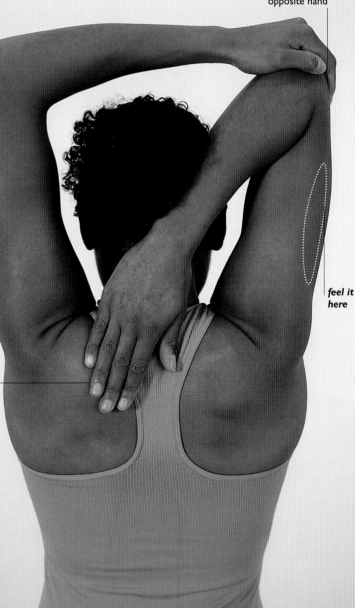

pull with opposite hand

feel it here

reach hand between shoulder blades

1 Raise your right hand up and reach it over your head, aiming to touch between your shoulder blades.

2 Move your left hand up behind your head, take hold of your right elbow, and press down. Hold this position for 5–10 seconds, then rest. Switch arms. Repeat twice on each side.

BACK STRETCH

This stretch helps to loosen the erector spinae, which are the muscles that run down either side of the spine. It also helps relax the lower back. If you suffer from muscular tension in this area, it's a good idea to perform this stretch every day, and in place of the back extension (*see p59*), which strengthens the back, but may aggravate tightness.

legs at 90° angle

1 Lie flat on your back and bend your knees up towards your chest, so that your knees are bent at a 90° angle. Rest your arms by your sides, and keep your lower back flat, pressing your spine into the mat.

2 Place your hands behind your knees and pull the backs of your thighs into your chest. Let your back sink into the mat. Hold this position for 20–30 seconds, then relax. Repeat twice. Release your legs and slowly lower them to the ground.

pull thighs towards body

feel it here

RESISTANCE TRAINING

It is important that you incorporate resistance training into your running programme, no matter what your age. The routines do not have to be complicated and, as with running, consistency is much more important than perfection. I recommend using the resistance training routine on pages 52–59 as an introduction to resistance training. Perform these eight exercises regularly in any order you find convenient, giving yourself a comfortable number of rest days in between.

Why use resistance training?

Most competitive long-distance runners supplement their running programme with resistance training. The increased muscular power it yields, particularly in the lower body, gives runners a competitive edge while racing. In other words, more muscle strength will probably enable them to run a bit faster over the last 400 metres (¼ mile) of a race and helps delay the muscular fatigue that causes runners to go anaerobic. These benefits are universal, and anyone, from the beginner to the professional runner, can use resistance training to boost their running performance.

Striking a balance to avoid injury

Another benefit of resistance training involves body balance, which running and daily strains can cause to fall out of healthy proportion. Certain opposing muscle groups, such as the quadriceps and hamstrings, should fall within a certain range of relative strength. The ratio of strength should be roughly 60 per cent in the quadriceps to 40 per cent in the hamstrings. Maintaining this ratio is good insurance against injury, since it prevents either set of muscles from bearing the brunt of your running.

Resistance training also helps assure a left–right side balance of as close to 50 per cent to 50 per cent as possible, which also helps to guard against injury in much the same way. Not only does a balanced physique guard against potential injury, but it looks great too.

THE BENEFITS OF RESISTANCE TRAINING

Weight training is the perfect form of exercise to complement your running programme. Here are just a few of the benefits:

- a more attractive, streamlined body

- increased basal metabolic rate, both during exercise and well into rest and recovery

- increased base running pace

- delayed atrophy of muscles associated with ageing

- prevention of injury by strengthening muscles around joints and balancing muscle ratio

- better posture and muscular longevity

Looking good at any age

Resistance training will yield fast results in improving the appearance of your body. Everyone's muscles atrophy with age; this is a fact, even in relatively active people. After the age of 35, both men and women lose muscle mass at a rate of about 1.4kg (3 pounds) per decade, which can lead to a whole range of health problems, from a decrease in your metabolic rate to stooped posture.

The good news is that consistent resistance training can slow the process of muscular atrophy, and the earlier you get started, the better it is for your muscular longevity. It certainly helps your self-image to look in the mirror and see good posture and lean muscle definition, both of which are pleasant side benefits of resistance training. When done consistently, and in conjunction with a fat-burning running regimen, resistance training can give you your most attractive, streamlined body yet.

Your optimum weight and repetitions

The weight of your dumbbells and the number of repetitions or "reps" you perform depends not only on your base muscular strength, but also on what you want to achieve. For lean, toned muscles, it's best to focus on a high number of repetitions with light weights. If your aim is to bulk up your muscles, you should perform relatively few repetitions, but with heavy weights.

A good starting point is to begin with 8–12 reps. For toned muscles, the perfect weight to lift should leave you able to do eleven reps at 60–80 per cent of your maximum muscular effort, and at 100 per cent effort by the twelfth. To build up muscle mass, aim to lift weights that allow you to perform seven reps at 60–80 per cent of maximum, and the eighth at 100 per cent effort. The goal is to eventually do this number of reps three separate times in what are called "sets."

Work up to three sets of 8–12 repetitions, with a 30-second recovery period in between each one. At first, you may need to rest for as much as 1–2 minutes. Depending on your needs, increase the weight you're lifting when you find yourself capable of doing more than three sets of 8–12 reps.

Frequency and effort

Rest days are essential in resistance training. You should therefore avoid exercising the same muscles every day. A good rule of thumb is to train with weights only every other day, or even every third or fourth day, in order to give your impaired muscles

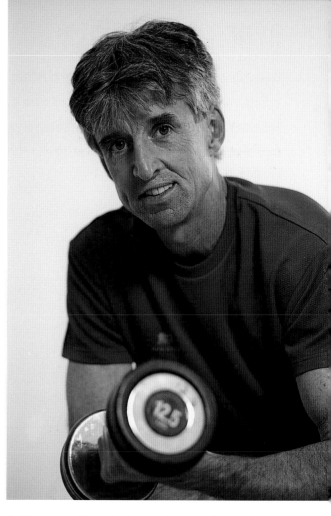

As I have aged, I have also increased my overall strength: I am not as fast a runner as I was when I was 25, but I am physically stronger. It has been very satisfying from a goal-setting perspective to be able to actually see improvements in my strength and appearance.

the ability to rebuild torn-down muscle fibres and resist injury. Perform the exercises on pages 52–59 in any order you wish, and do not be afraid to listen to your body to determine how many recovery days you need between performing them.

Remember, you are not aiming to become a bodybuilder. Resistance training should complement your running, not overtake it.

BENCH PRESS WITH DUMBBELLS

This exercise works both the pectorals in the chest and the triceps in the backs of the upper arms. An excellent addition to your running programme, the bench press will define the upper body muscles, which lend themselves to a strong and balanced-looking physique. If you prefer to do the bench press with a barbell, always have another person there to "spot" or help you.

palms face forwards

1 Lie on your back on a bench with your knees bent. Hold your feet together and rest them on the end of the bench. Take a dumbbell in each hand and keep your palms facing forwards. Position your arms so that your elbows are bent at right angles. Keep your back flat and pressed into the bench: arching your back can put undue stress on your lower back.

feel it here

2 Extend your arms slowly straight up from your chest, making sure you don't lock your arms in the process. To maximize the effectiveness of this movement, pretend you are squeezing a large ball between your upper arms as you extend. Exhale as you extend them upwards, then inhale as you bring your arms back to the start position. Perform 1–3 sets of 8–12 repetitions each.

BICEPS CURL WITH DUMBBELLS

Perhaps the best-known muscles in the human body, the biceps are located in the fronts of the upper arms. Ironically, they are often overlooked, but without them, you could not lift a shopping bag or even pump your arms while running. When done in conjunction with the bench press (*see opposite*), this exercise will give you a lean and toned upper body.

lean upper body forwards

feel it here

1 Sit on the edge of a chair or bench with your feet shoulder-width apart. Lean forwards slightly and place your left elbow on your left thigh, resting the left hand on the right thigh. Grasp a dumbbell in your right hand and extend the arm, letting the side of your arm rest against your right thigh for support.

2 Bend in the extended arm slowly, feeling the contraction in the biceps muscle in the front of the upper arm. Hold your stomach tight as you bend and extend your arm to complete one repetition. Exhale as you bend, and breathe in as you extend. Repeat this bend and extend motion up to 12 times. Perform 1–3 sets of 8–12 repetitions. Change sides and repeat.

SQUATS

The quadriceps, which are the large muscles located in the fronts of your thighs, and the gluteals, or buttock muscles, both play an integral part in your running performance. Strengthening them with squats can improve your pace and endurance, and give you long, lean thighs and a firm bottom. You can incorporate small hand-held dumbbells to advance this exercise if you wish.

feet
hip-width
apart

arms rise up

feel it here

feel it here

1 Stand with your feet hip-width apart and your toes pointing forwards. Hold your arms relaxed at your sides and tighten your stomach as you prepare to descend. To concentrate more on the gluteals than the thighs, turn your toes inwards.

2 Lean your upper body forwards and let your arms rise up to shoulder height as you bend your knees to squat down. This arm motion will help your balance as you descend. Take care not to squat too deeply, since this can cause damage to the knees. Exhale as you squat down, and inhale as you rise back up to the starting position. Perform 1–3 sets of 8–12 squats each.

HAMSTRING CURL

The hamstrings in the backs of your thighs are very important muscles in running – especially for propelling your body weight uphill. These muscles are often less developed than the quadriceps in the fronts of the thighs, and this off-kilter ratio can lead to injury. The following hamstring curl can correct this imbalance. Add small ankle weights if you wish to increase the resistance.

1 Kneel face down on the ground and form a bridge with your body on your elbows and knees. Support your upper body with your elbows, and extend your right leg straight out behind you at just above hip height.

extend leg just above hip height

curl leg in

feel it here

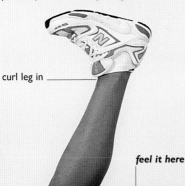

2 Bend your right leg in towards your bottom and then slowly extend it out to the starting position. Think of this as the biceps curl for the lower body: it uses the same controlled motion to isolate the hamstrings. You should feel the burn in the back of the leg. Perform 1–3 sets of 8–12 repetitions. Change sides and repeat.

ADDUCTOR LIFT

The adductors are commonly referred to as the inner thigh muscles, and they play a key role in preventing many injuries, such as groin strain. They are difficult to isolate and are often neglected in resistance training, so this exercise is particularly useful. To intensify the work of the inner thigh, add small ankle weights when performing the adductor lift.

1 Lie on your right side and bend your top leg over your bottom leg. Your left leg should form a bridge over your right leg, with your left foot planted squarely on the floor in front of you. Keep your right leg straight with your foot flexed.

left foot in front of body

2 Lift your right leg up as high as you can, leading with your heel. Hold this position for three counts, and then lower your leg down just above the mat. You should feel a burn in your upper inner thigh. Perform 1–3 sets of 8–12 repetitions. Change sides and repeat.

lead with heel

feel it here

ABDUCTOR LIFT

The abductor muscles are located in the hips, and they are responsible for "abducting" the legs away from the body. Target these muscles by performing the following hip-toning exercise either with or without ankle weights. This exercise will complement your fat-burning running routine to give you sleek, lean hips, as well as toned, strong outer thighs.

support head
with hand

1 Lie on your left side with one leg stacked directly on top of the other. Place your right hand, palm down, in front of you to brace yourself. Support your head on your left hand.

2 Lift your right leg upwards in a slow motion, holding it there for a count of three. Slowly bring your right leg back down so that it hovers just above your left leg. You should feel your outer thigh and hip working. Perform 1–3 sets of 8–12 repetitions. Change sides and repeat.

hold for 3 seconds

feel it here

ABDOMINAL CRUNCHES

The stomach muscles are also known as the abdominals, and keeping yours strong can help to prevent back problems. Strong abdominals also support upright posture, which can make the body appear tall and elongated. The following exercise is particularly useful in preventing back strain and "stitches", or cramps in the sides of the abdominals that sometimes occur while running.

feet hip-width apart

1 Lie on your back on a mat or carpet with your legs bent, feet hip-width apart. Place your hands behind the base of your head, so that you are lightly supporting your neck. Keep your elbows wide out to the sides and your chin lifted.

2 Curl your upper body up off the mat, taking care not to use your arms to pull yourself up. The contraction of your stomach muscles should be enough to lift your torso slightly. Press your lower back into the mat and exhale as you curl up. Inhale as you lower yourself back down onto the mat. Your range of motion should be small, but the muscle contraction in your abdominals should be intense. Perform 1–3 sets of 15 crunches each.

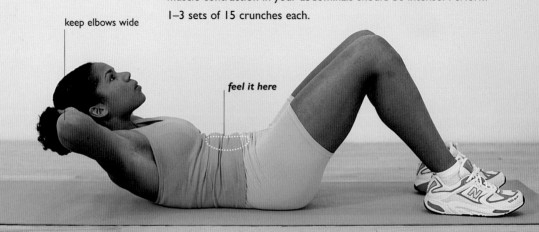

keep elbows wide

feel it here

BACK EXTENSION

Back pain is a common complaint among runners. The first line of defence should be to strengthen the muscles that run alongside the spine, also called the erector spinae. When performed in conjunction with the abdominal crunches (*see opposite*) and the back stretch (*see p49*), this exercise will strengthen the core of the body, and thereby alleviate strain on the muscles in the back.

1 Lie flat on your stomach on a mat or carpet. Bend your arms out to the sides, placing your hands, palms down, just beneath your chin.

2 Use your back muscles to lift your arms and chest up off the mat slightly, exhaling as you do so. Hold this raised position for three seconds, and inhale as you lower your torso to the ground. This exercise does not require a large range of motion, but it must be performed in a slow and precise manner for maximum results. Perform 1–3 sets of 15 back extensions each.

hold for 3 seconds

feel it here

WARM-UP AND STRETCH

A regular stretching routine can help prevent injury while leaving your body lithe and limber. Perform the stretches below (*for instructions, see pp42–49*) in any order you wish. One caveat: always make sure your muscles are warmed up properly before stretching.

Warm-up [*see p38*]

Walk or jog at a slowed-down pace (*for your optimum warm-up pace, see box, p38*) for at least five minutes to warm up your muscles before your training run.

To prevent straining cold muscles, perform the following stretches in any order after your run or, at the very least, after your warm-up walk or jog.

Jog slowly for 5–10 minutes

Hamstring and calf stretch *p42*

Hip, back, and side stretch *p43*

Hip stretch I *p44*

Hip stretch II *p45*

Lying quadriceps stretch *p46*

Standing calf stretch *p47*   Triceps stretch *p48*

Back stretch *p49*

STRENGTHEN AND COOL-DOWN

Always jog slowly or walk for a few minutes to allow your body to cool down after you run. On days you do not run, integrate the following resistance exercises (*for instructions, see pp52–59*) in any order for a balanced and streamlined physique. Be sure to stretch afterwards, though.

Bench press with dumbbells *p52*

Biceps curl with dumbbells *p53*

Squats *p54*

Hamstring curl *p55*

Adductor lift *p56*

Abductor lift *p57*

Abdominal crunches *p58*

Back extension *p59*

Jog slowly for 5–10 minutes

Cool-down (*see p40*)

You should always walk or jog slowly after your run to cool down. After a hard run, which could be a race, a long run of more than 90 minutes, interval training (see pp112–17), or hill training (see pp118–19), cool down for at least ten minutes. For easy runs that do not involve going anaerobic, cool down for up to five minutes.

MASSAGE AND FOAM ROLLING

Muscle tissue can become tight with overuse, forming tight "knots" that can be painful or even lead to injury over time. Professional athletes will have regular deep-tissue massages to relax these knots and keep their muscle tissue in peak condition, but the cost of hiring a masseur after each run would be prohibitive to most everyday runners. Foam rollers provide a low-cost alternative, allowing you to use your own body weight to apply controlled pressure to specific muscle groups as often as required.

When to use a foam roller

You do not need to use a roller every time you exercise. Pay attention to your body: when you feel "knots" of tension build in your muscles, it is time to try using a roller to release that tension. If you wish, you can also use your roller before exercising to loosen up a particular set of musles, or after a long run to help break down the lactic acid which can build up within your muscles and cause soreness. Foam rollers may also be used as part of an injury recovery programme; make sure to consult your doctor or physiotherapist before using a roller for this purpose.

How to use a roller

Once you have located an area of tension, roll forwards and backwards over the area for a minimum of 30 seconds (less if you are using the roller to warm up your muscles). Pause over any sensitive points, holding your position until the discomfort eases and relaxes completely. Breathe normally as you roll, and avoid rolling over any bony areas, such as the ankle or hip. Repeat the exercise on the other side of the body, even if the tension is only on one side (for instance, in one leg), to prevent muscle imbalances. Remember: as you roll, it should be your body doing all the work, not the roller.

CHOOSING A FOAM ROLLER

Foam rollers are typically about 15cm (6in) in diameter, and are available in a variety of lengths, from 30cm (1ft) to 90cm (3ft) long. The ideal length for a first roller is about 45cm (18in), as they are large enough to cope with a variety of exercises but still short enough to store easily.

Rollers are available in a variety of different densities, textures, and shapes. Density and texture affect the pressure and intensity of the massage, while half-rollers and other unusually shaped pieces of equipment can be used for specific types of massage. For basic massage, choose a simple round roller with a medium density.

Sports balls can also be used to concentrate massage on a single area, like the sole of the foot (see p105).

Outer-leg roller exercise

By using the general method described opposite, runners can use foam rollers to massage muscle groups throughout the body. For example, the exercise below is designed to help loosen outer-leg tissue, including the iliotibial band (see p100). Runners are especially prone to tightness in this area.

Keep lower leg straight and raised off the ground

1 Lie on your left side, with the roller just above your knee. Support your upper body on your left forearm and place the other hand on your hip. Cross your right leg over the left, and put your right foot flat on the floor.

2 Using your left arm, gently push down over the roller, until it is level with the top of your thigh, then pull back up until it is above your knee again. Repeat for 30 seconds. Turn over and massage your right leg.

feel it here

push with your arm

THE SUPPORT SYSTEM

ON A BRISK AUTUMN AFTERNOON, I SHOWED UP ON MY UNIVERSITY'S ATHLETIC FIELDS FOR MY FIRST CROSS-COUNTRY PRACTICE. I WAS READY TO RACE OVER HILL AND DALE; TO ME, TRAINING MEANT RUNNING HARD. GIEG WAS THERE IN HIS CAR WITH THE MOTOR RUNNING, WATCHING THE TEAM RUN FROM THE WARMTH OF HIS STEEL COCOON. OCCASIONALLY HE WOULD ROLL DOWN THE WINDOW TO TELL US TO "WUN EASY AND WEELAX." THIS WAS MY INTRODUCTION TO GIEG'S IDEA THAT THERE'S MORE TO ACHIEVING PEAK CARDIOVASCULAR FITNESS THAN TRAINING HARD ALL THE TIME.

YOUR PHYSIOLOGY AND RUNNING

Running is different from other aerobic exercise in that the trauma of pounding puts more stress on your musculoskeletal system than do lower-impact activities. This trauma also adversely affects your red blood cell count, your bones, and your connective tissue. However, you can use some of the tips and information listed in this chapter to tailor your training to facilitate faster recovery and avoid overtraining.

Your body and overtraining

Overtraining is a chronic condition brought on by long-term under-recovery. It is characterized by muscular fatigue, soreness, and feeling burned out. Do not confuse overtraining with being tired for a few days; it is a downward spiral, where your ability to train continues to deteriorate.

If you do not give your body enough time to rest between workouts, you are probably overtraining. This impedes you from improving performance as quickly as you might have done had you included very easy recovery days into your routine. You might think that you are getting stronger, but your body will feel weak and your runs laboured. Over time, your body simply breaks down and succumbs to this subtle and constant lack of total recovery in your routine.

How will I know if I'm overtraining?

The good news is that overtraining usually occurs after a long period of time, so it is rarely a problem for new runners. However, if you are an intermediate to advanced runner, or if you simply want a more concrete way to determine if you are overtraining, let your pulse be your guide. One sign of over-training can be an elevation of your resting heart rate (RHR) over time. An increased RHR, or your pulse at a time when you are supposed to be calm, is an indication that your body is being overworked, and more rest and less hard running are in order. You may want to take your resting pulse at the same

KNOW YOUR BODY

The repetitive pounding in running exposes skeletal weaknesses, which we all have. This is why one runner might have chronic knee problems, while another might struggle with his or her hips, feet, or iliotibial band. However, even the most heavy-footed, orthopaedically challenged person can become a fast, strong runner if they acknowledge their need for a bit more time for recovery than their light-footed counterparts.

For example, Olympic marathon runner Kenny Moore always took two easy days between his hard workouts to my one, but our hard training was essentially the same. We both achieved the same Olympic level, since what matters in increasing performance is the intensity and consistency of your hard workouts, not the number of easy days in between. It is the hard training that will increase your racing speed, so take as many easy days as your body needs to regenerate between hard sessions. Just be honest with yourself and tailor your training to live with it.

time every morning and write it down, like I do. If you find that your resting pulse over a given period has risen by about ten beats per minute on average, then you may be overtraining.

Healing is a matter of simple cell division

Your body generally needs 24–48 hours to heal or recover from the trauma of a very hard run (see *opposite*), depending on your body's rate of cell division and your own unique physiological makeup. During a run, your feet and legs absorb the impact of up to four times your body weight, and this creates microscopic tears in the leg muscle fibres. In addition, this pounding also puts strain on your bones and connective tissue, and destroys some red blood cells, which need to be replaced. If you do not allow your body the time to recover, you could be on the road to overtraining.

The "very hard/very easy" rule

This is my personal rule of training, which reminds me that I always improve the most when I give myself time to recover between hard training sessions. The very hard/very easy rule will also take you a long way towards avoiding overtraining. It involves taking a very easy day after every hard workout in order to allow the body to regenerate. The very easy day following your very hard day of training is absolutely essential for the regeneration of your body: your muscles, bone and blood cells, and connective tissue immediately begin to heal themselves following your hard run. Some people may even need two easy days between hard workouts in order to complete this process of regeneration. Be sure to listen to your body – if you continue to overtrain, or train hard at the level of intensity that tore down your muscles in the first place, your body will never heal completely.

What is "very hard" and "very easy"?

Your very hard and very easy days are relative to your level of fitness. As a beginner, run only every other day, taking a complete rest day in between. Take a walk instead, or play with your children. Whatever you do, it should be an easy activity for you. Since your hard run at this level should never go beyond conversational pace, which is necessarily within your own personal aerobic threshold, it should be very difficult for you to overtrain.

As you improve to intermediate and advanced levels, you may be running every day. On your very hard day you might add some extra time to your base run, or maybe even incorporate some interval training (see pp112–17) into your workout. For your easy day, you might run a familiar loop at conversational pace. As you get fitter, your hard days should become relatively harder and your easy days relatively easier. Time your very easy runs if you wish. My training group always went at the pace of the person who felt like going the slowest on the day.

The friction coefficient and recovery

Some runners are lighter on their feet than others, which is due to their varying friction coefficients. Knowing yours won't help you recover more quickly than before: it simply explains why you may need more easy days than your running partner. Simply put, this is the energy used to propel the body forwards, relative to that which is lost and pushed downwards into the ground. It's not just down to body weight, either. Even light-weight runners can have a heavy footstrike. "Landing hard" produces more microtears in your leg muscle fibres than being light-footed, and therefore the body requires extra time to recover and regenerate.

TRAINING AT AN OLYMPIC LEVEL

No matter your ability, every runner needs to strike a careful balance between very hard and and very easy training sessions.

When training for the Olympic marathon, I ran twice a day every day except Sunday, when I ran 20 miles (32km). While this may seem like a lot, only three of my sessions, including the Sunday run, were very hard. The remaining ten sessions were very easy, giving my body plenty of time to recover.

GENERAL MOTIVATION

The human brain is the most sophisticated organ in the body. It is therefore not surprising that, for many competitive athletes, mental preparation is almost as important as physical training. Athletes often develop routines to help them focus their minds and block out distractions. Try incorporating the following sports psychology tools into your training, from visualization to positive ritual, and you will see an overall improvement in your performance.

Visualization

Years ago, researchers discovered a thought process they called visualization, and it was common and instinctive to successful people, no matter what their competitive discipline. For runners, visualization can be used anytime, but it is particularly beneficial when preparing for a competition. Visualization is not a mysterious training trick – it is merely the act of imagining yourself being successful in the situation for which you are preparing. Simply "see" yourself running a strong race in the future. This should not be a constant thought process: just have a future goal at the back of your mind and every now and then, think about yourself in that situation and imagine yourself achieving your goal successfully. The confidence it gives you will not only allow you to relax during your training workouts, but it will also help you to feel more secure about the race itself. The best way to describe the result is that you will get to a critical point in your event – such as kilometre 32.2 (mile 20) in a marathon – and you will feel as though you have been there before.

VISUALIZATION TO VICTORY

While training for the Olympics, I often imagined myself feeling strong at the crucial point of the marathon. I attached the thought of that moment in my future to my current effort. It was always at the back of my mind. The eventual result is that during the race, I felt as if I had been there before: a hypersensitive *déjà vu*.

This familiarity with the "real time" moment allowed me to feel relaxed and confident that I was doing it right. At the 14.5-km (9-mile) point of the 1972 Olympic marathon, when I found myself actually there in real time, pulling away from the field, I felt chills over my entire body. I felt that what was happening should be happening. For some reason, I knew everyone else in the race was in trouble.

Achieve your goals to boost confidence

Hitting your set targets will bolster your confidence and inspire you to perform your best. "Reasonable," "incremental," and "attainable" are the words that have shaped my goals for the forty-plus years I have been a runner. Being reasonable means being realistic: ask yourself, how are you truly feeling that day? Have you recovered completely from your previous workout? The answers to these questions should always be factors in deciding what you are capable of achieving on a particular day. If your goal is attainable, you will be able to complete your run successfully even if your physical and emotional energies are at their lowest. Then you can always finish your workout (and maybe even do just a little bit more than you had planned). This successful completion of your goals will yield psychological reinforcement, and this will benefit your physical performance.

The power of positive ritual

Positive ritual involves developing a routine that remains standard and consistent throughout your training regimen. It may be something as simple as brushing your teeth before you begin your run. In fact, it can be anything, so long as you do it every time you train. Then, when you are in a stressful situation, such as a race, this positive ritual tells your subconscious that you are embarking on a training run; that you have done this before. Not surprisingly, this has a huge impact on your mood, allowing you to relax, and subsequently improve your performance.

There are many ways you can incorporate positive ritual into your training – you could even "ritually" tie your shoe. In 1972, the world record holder in the steeplechase track event accidentally kicked off his spike when his shoelace came untied, only to plant his wet, bare foot at the base of the next hurdle and slide into it, and out of the Olympic final. Today, many runners still ritually double-knot their shoes just before they run.

Reset your mind with positive ritual: double-knot your shoe each time you go out for a run as a form of positive ritual.

TRAINING LOGS

A training log is one of the most practical tools you can use in becoming your own coach. Keeping a log of your workouts is essential for monitoring your performance and tracking your improvement. It gives you an accurate idea of where you were when you started, and how you have progressed from there in terms of fitness and motivation. It is also useful in determining what type of regimen works best for you. Many running apps record and log your training automatically, or you can write out your own log if you prefer.

Why keep a log?

A log is valuable for many reasons. It will force you to be honest with yourself as you set your reasonable, incremental, and attainable goals. When working solely from memory, I seem to subtract some time when I run for speed; when I run for distance, I may add a little extra. These little white lies are a natural tendency, but they can skew your data and prevent you from setting your optimum goals, which can thwart your progress.

Training logs are wonderful tools for recording what you have achieved. You can look back and take stock of your progress and the physical and emotional state you were in at the time.

How to keep a log

If you use a fitness tracker or app, basic information about your runs, including distance and pace, will probably be recorded automatically. Depending on the type of device, you may be able to supplement your log with additional information, such as other exercise you have done (such as resistance training or gym visits) or the food you have consumed.

If you prefer to write a log yourself, remember to record the date, the time, distance, and your emotional and physiological state. I normally write down my results for the day, sometimes with a brief comment or two. Although my training is advanced, my logs are not that different from those of a beginner (see below for an example log).

FRANK'S SAMPLE LOG (AGED 45)

Monday, October 11:	7:00 a.m. 7 miles	3:00 p.m. 6 × 800 metres in 2:24; last in 2:21	*felt sharp*
Tuesday, October 12:	7:00 a.m. 6 miles (easy)	3:00 p.m. 7 miles on trails	*felt sluggish*
Wednesday, October 13:	7:00 a.m. 5 miles on bike	3:00 p.m. 9-mile run (easy)	*felt good*
Thursday, October 14:	7:00 a.m. 6 miles (very easy)	3:00 p.m. 12 × 400 metres in 71; last in 68	*felt good*
Friday, October 15:	7:00 a.m. 7-mile trail run	3:00 p.m. 7-mile campus run	*loose, but tired*
Saturday, October 16:	10:00 a.m. 5km race (15:20)	3:00 p.m. 5 miles (easy run)	*felt good*
Sunday, October 17:	7:00 a.m.–9:00 a.m. 2-hour run (60% MHR); 15–17 miles		*felt strong*

NB: 1.6km = 1 mile; 400 metres = ¼ mile

FITTING IT INTO YOUR WEEK

One of the biggest challenges running presents is finding a way to fit it into your busy day. There are lots of things and people that should take precedence over your running regimen, from work to the kids to socializing with friends. However, with a little planning, ingenuity, and lateral thinking, you can find time for everything, including your running programme. Read on for some valuable multi-tasking and time-saving tips that will add hours to your day.

Become an early riser

If you're a full-time parent, make the most of your early mornings! Lying in bed for that extra half-hour may feel great at the time, but it doesn't actually make much difference to how rested you are throughout the day. Try going to bed just 30 minutes earlier than you would normally, so you can use that found time for an early-morning run. A morning run will leave you feeling positive and energized for the rest of the day, and you'll never have to worry about fitting your runs around your schedule (or vice versa).

Multi-tasking for extra time

Do you live within a reasonable distance from your workplace? If so, running to work in the morning might be an option. This is a great way to get some exercise, energize yourself, and clear your head before you start your workday. It also cuts down on transportation costs and emissions, contributing to a cleaner environment.

Many large companies have showers on the premises, so check with your Human Resources department first to find out where they are and if they provide soap and towels. If your company does not have showers, you might simply consider running home after work, which will help relieve the stress of the workday, while also creating personal time and saving money.

Multi-tasking for found time: invest in a small rucksack to wear while running to or from your workplace.

Exercising during your lunch break is another option for the time-pressed runner. A 30-minute run can ease the tension of the day, leaving you feeling refreshed and ready to face the afternoon's workload. Just make sure there is a shower in your building; or join a nearby gym and run and shower there.

NUTRITION

Eating a balanced diet is vitally important for a runner. As well as knowing which food groups you should be eating from and when, it's useful to understand how different vitamins and minerals can affect your health. Some are important for promoting healthy bone development, while others lower your blood pressure, or ensure that you recover from injuries quickly. Your diet should include as much unprocessed food as possible; only use energy bars or sports drinks when you really need a boost, before or during training.

A healthy diet

There are five main food groups everyone should aim to eat every day for optimum energy and health: carbohydrates, protein, fruits and vegetables, dairy products, and healthy fats and oils. A good diet should include a certain amount of servings of each food group, and each group performs key tasks within the body (see below): what we eat not only fuels us, but also repairs and protects us. For runners, who push their bodies to the limit, maintaining a balanced diet is especially important.

Energy and glycogen

Carbohydrates are the source of the body's energy. When we digest carbohydrates, they are converted to glucose and transported to our cells by the hormone insulin, ready for our bodies to use.

THE FIVE FOOD GROUPS

Food group	Advantages	Good Sources	How much per day
Carbohydrates	Provide energy for muscles, reducing fatigue. Help to curb hunger, so healthy choices here can help if you want to reduce your body weight.	Wholegrain rice, pasta, bread, bagels, and cereals; rye/stoneground wheat crackers, sweet potatoes, quinoa, polenta.	6–11 servings
Protein	Rich in amino acids, which promote muscle growth and healing. Darker meats are richer in iron and zinc.	Meat, poultry, eggs, peanut butter, tinned beans, fish, tofu.	2–3 servings
Fruit and vegetables	Provide an excellent source of vitamins and minerals, which help promote healing post-exercise (see pp74–75). Also a source of carbohydrates and fibre.	Fruit: citrus fruits (such as oranges, limes, grapefruits, tangerines), bananas, berries, melon, kiwi. Vegetables: salad leaves, "greens" such as broccoli, kale, and spinach, peppers (red, green, and yellow). The more variety the better.	5+ servings
Dairy products	Help maintain strong bones and reduce the risk of osteoporosis. A good source of protein. Rich in calcium, vitamin D, potassium, phosphorus, and riboflavin.	Low-fat milk, cheeses, yoghurt.	2–3 servings
Healthy fats and oils	The "good" fats are omega-3, -6 and -9. These support the immune system, nerve activity, and brain function, and help the body process vitamins.	Omega-3: oily fish, mussels; omega-6: walnut, olive, sunflower, grapeseed oils; omega-9: almonds, avocados, olives, pecans.	Moderate amounts of "healthy fats".

THE GLYCAEMIC INDEX

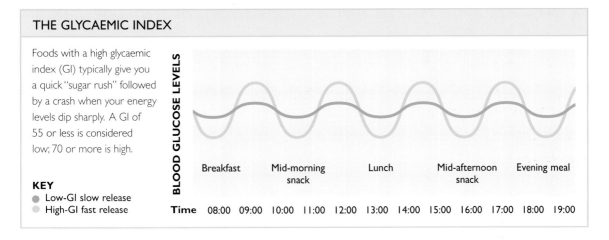

Foods with a high glycaemic index (GI) typically give you a quick "sugar rush" followed by a crash when your energy levels dip sharply. A GI of 55 or less is considered low; 70 or more is high.

KEY
- Low-GI slow release
- High-GI fast release

BLOOD GLUCOSE LEVELS

Breakfast   Mid-morning snack   Lunch   Mid-afternoon snack   Evening meal

Time   08:00   09:00   10:00   11:00   12:00   13:00   14:00   15:00   16:00   17:00   18:00   19:00

If there is too much glucose in the body, it is stored in the muscles and liver as glycogen.

Not all carbohydrates are equal, however. Nutritionists use the glycaemic index (GI) to determine the speed at which different carbohydrates are converted into energy, rating them on a scale from 1–100. Low-GI foods are broken down at a slower rate than high-GI foods. A GI below 55 is considered low, and can encompass foods which are sometimes known as "complex" carbohydrates (such as wholegrain bread and brown rice) alongside some fruits, vegetables, and legumes. These foods release energy slowly, keeping your blood glucose levels fairly even throughout the day (see box, above). They also leave you feeling fuller, meaning that you are less likely to want to snack impulsively.

At the other end of the scale, high-GI foods (over 70) break down and release energy fast, and are sometimes referred to as "simple" carbohydrates for this reason. White bread and rice, potatoes, and foods high in sugar fall into the high-GI category. Eating these foods can cause your blood sugar to spike (sometimes known as a "sugar rush") and then drop quickly as those stores of energy deplete. For this reason, high-GI foods are often regarded as being less healthy than low-GI foods, especially since high-GI foods tend to be higher in calories and,

in the case of sugary snacks and drinks, lack nutritional benefit. This is not always the case – a banana can be a healthy snack, in spite of the fact that it is a high-GI food (with a score of 62), because it is also a great source of potassium and fibre. High-GI foods can feature in a balanced diet, as long as they are of nutritional benefit.

Fuel your training

Most people can store around 2,000kcal (8,400kJ) of glycogen in their body, enough to power a run of around 20 miles. This can pose a challenge for runners training for long-distance events like marathons, because once these stores are entirely depleted, you become extremely tired – commonly referred to as "hitting the wall" (see box, p135).

You can train your body over time to delay reaching this stage, allowing you to run further and longer without experiencing an energy crash. The secret is to condition your body to use fat as fuel once your glycogen reserves run low. To achieve this, you need to train at an easy, low-intensity level for longer periods of time to increase your overall stamina. You also need to adapt your diet, cutting back on high-GI foods and increasing your intake of proteins and healthy fats (check with your doctor first before making changes to your diet).

If you are used to a diet high in sugar and simple carbohydrates, these changes may take some discipline, but it will help you become leaner, stronger, and fitter in the long run.

Most importantly, with these training and dietary changes your muscles will be able to hold increased amounts of glycogen and, once those supplies run out, your body will become used to using fat as fuel. Once your stamina has noticeably improved during low-intensity training sessions, you can then gradually increase the intensity of your runs. You can also prepare yourself for an even greater fuel boost in the days leading up to a big race using a strategy known as "carbo-loading" (see p135).

Energy-rich snacks and sports drinks

Even if you have conditioned your body and are able to push yourself further on your glycogen stores, it may still not be enough to carry you to the finish line, especially during longer runs and races. In these instances, you may want to use high-GI sports bars or drinks to give yourself a boost. Packed with sugar, they are designed to provide a spike in energy right when you need it most. Sports drinks also tend to contain electrolytes, salt-based minerals to replace those that are lost as you sweat.

Commercially made sports bars often focus only on the sugar content, and otherwise contain little nutritional benefit. To avoid this problem you might want to consider making your own energy-rich bars and snacks, using a blend of high-GI fruits, nuts, and seeds. Of course, the best option for a portable, high-energy snack is also the simplest one: a piece of fruit. Likewise, you do not need to buy expensive sports drinks every time you train: de-fizzed cola can be used as an energy boost, or else a bottle of water with a little rock or table salt will help to replenish electrolytes (see *Hydration*, pp76–77).

Make sure that you time your energy boost well in order to feel its benefits. Energy bars and snacks should be eaten no later than an hour before a run or race, in order to give it time to be digested. It is no use eating a sports bar while you are running: the food will only sit in your stomach and weigh you down, and not provide the necessary energy in time. Sip sports drinks at regular intervals during your runs, rather than gulping them down. You do not want a lot of liquid sloshing around inside you as you run.

Do not believe that, as a runner, consuming commercial sports bars and drinks on a regular basis will give you an edge. They should be used sparingly, and only during training (or before, in the case of snacks). Remember to factor the high sugar content (and therefore high-GI) of these snacks and drinks into the rest of your day's diet, balancing them out with plenty of low-GI foods.

Strengthen and repair

A healthy and varied diet should not only energize you, but also keep your body in top condition. Protein is essential for keeping your muscles in good repair. Meat, poultry, fish, and legumes all contain amino acids, which help to regenerate muscle tissue after they have been torn down during exercise. Aim for between three to five servings of protein a day, preferably from a variety of different sources.

Vitamins and minerals also perform key roles in keeping your body at its best (see *opposite*). Proteins and carbohydrates are a good source for certain nutrients, such as red meat for iron, while many others are found in a variety of different food groups. Vitamin C, for instance, helps to keep connective tissue healthy. A portion of berries or an orange are both great sources of Vitamin C – snack on these and you may find yourself at a reduced risk of strained or sprained tendons.

Calcium is also vital for runners: it builds bone strength, thereby reducing the incidence of fractures and other similar injuries. Dairy products are known for being rich in calcium; if you are lactose intolerant, look out for fortified plant-based milk substitutes instead. In order for the body to fully absorb calcium, you also need a regular intake of Vitamin D. As well as being found in oily fish, dairy, and eggs, sunlight can also provide this vitamin through exposed skin. It's the one vitamin you can get simply by going for a run on a sunny day – just remember to put on sunscreen first.

Supplements

As their name implies, supplements top up the body with an additional boost of vitamins and minerals. In theory, if you eat a healthy, balanced diet rich in all the essential nutrients (see below), you should not need them at all.

That being said, very few people actually consume 100 per cent of the recommended daily allowances (RDA) of vitamins and minerals through their diet alone. As such, taking a daily multivitamin can help top up the body's stores of vitamins and minerals and keep it in peak running condition, provided that they are used as an addition to your diet, rather than as a replacement for healthy eating. Speak to your doctor or sports nutritionist before introducing supplements into your diet.

A word of caution, however. While supplements can be a wonderful addition to a person's exercise programme with the right guidance, they are not always highly regulated. In the United States, for instance, they are classed as food items, rather than drugs, meaning that there is less legislation governing what supplements can contain. While the choice to take supplements is always an individual decision, I recommend that anyone who is considering taking supplements should go to the UK Anti-Doping (UKAD) website. The site is continually updated, and lists any medications or supplements which have the potential to illegally enhance an athlete's performance, or may even be harmful to their health.

VITAMINS AND MINERALS

Nutrient	Advantages	Good Sources
Calcium	Promotes healthy bone development, regulates muscle contractions, supports blood clotting.	Dairy products, leafy greens, tofu, fortified flour, soya beans, fish bones (as in sardines or anchovies).
Iron	A key element in making new red blood cells, which carry oxygen to the muscles.	Lean red meat, liver, nuts, leafy greens like spinach, brown rice, dried apricots, beans.
Vitamin D	Maintains healthy bones and teeth.	Sunshine on the skin. Oily fish, dairy, eggs, fortified breakfast cereals.
Vitamin E	Protects cell membranes, meaning cells are well-formed.	Leafy green vegetables, nuts and seeds, cereals, wheatgerm.
Folic acid	Keeps the central nervous system healthy. Combined with vitamin B12, helps to build red blood cells.	Leafy green vegetables, broccoli, Brussels sprouts, peas, asparagus, chickpeas, lentils, brown rice, citrus fruit.
Potassium	Lowers blood pressure, keeps the body's fluids in balance.	Pulses, nuts and seeds, bananas, seafood, turkey and chicken, beef, bread.
Vitamin C	Maintains healthy connective tissue and cells.	Citrus fruit, berries, broccoli, Brussels sprouts, potato.
Zinc	Helps make new cells and enzymes, and promotes wound healing.	Dairy, lean meat, shellfish, wheatgerm, bread.

HYDRATION

Staying hydrated is an essential part of maintaining a healthy body. Water makes up 50–60 per cent of your body weight, supplies your body with minerals, helps keep cells functioning at an optimum level, and flushes out toxins. Your body naturally takes in liquid from everything you eat and drink, so you only need to drink more water when you feel thirsty. Listen to your body: make sure you drink enough when you feel thirsty to avoid dehydration, but not too much that you over-hydrate.

Keep hydrated with water

Water is the world's most perfect beverage, since it costs nothing, contains zero calories, flushes waste products out of the body, supplies invaluable minerals, and helps keep cells functioning at an optimum level. Aim to consume the equivalent of six to eight 240ml (8fl oz) glasses of water every day.

Your running performance decreases when you are dehydrated, so it is absolutely crucial to drink

water during and after you work out. There is no need to buy bottled water – in most cases tap water is perfectly healthy and clean, but if you feel you must drink purified water, there are a number of inexpensive water filters that are widely available for home use.

Some people find that a little caffeine in the form of coffee or de-fizzed cola actually improves their running performance (see box, below left). However, caffeinated beverages, such as tea, coffee, or cola, can all contribute to dehydration. To counteract their diuretic effects, always consume an additional glass of water for each caffeinated beverage you drink.

A LITTLE CAFFEINE CAN HELP

When consumed in moderation, caffeine can actually help improve running performance. Some runners find that it makes them feel stronger during their run. One cup of coffee contains around 80mg of caffeine, enough to boost the performance of a 70kg (11st) runner.

Hydrating for a run

Always make sure that you are fully hydrated before a run. Drink 500ml–1 litre (¾–1¾ pints) of water between 60 and 90 minutes before you set off. This allows time for any excess fluid to be excreted from your body and avoids excess fluid sloshing about in your stomach while you are running. If you are fully hydrated and the weather is not too hot, you may be able to leave your water bottle at home for runs of less than 20–30 minutes. However, you should work out what you need during training sessions, and taking a water bottle allows you to monitor your own hydration strategy. Take three or four small sips (avoid big gulps) from your water bottle every 10 to 15 minutes, or more frequently in hotter weather.

Electrolytes and over-hydration

"Electrolytes" is another term for essential minerals in the body (see p75). These can be lost through sweat as you exercise. One way of replenishing electrolyte reserves during a run is to consume a small amount of salt: adding half a teaspoon of table or rock salt to a standard 500ml (16fl oz) bottle of water will provide the correct balance.

You can also buy commercial sports drinks that provide electrolytes, along with carbohydrates for energy. If you choose to drink these, take care to consume them at the right times; drinks with a low to medium glucose level can be drunk before or during training, while drinks with a high glucose level should only be consumed after your run, due to their high carbohydrate content. Don't forget to factor these drinks into your daily calorie count, particularly if you're running for weight loss.

While you should rehydrate yourself whenever you feel thirsty, be careful not to overdo it. Drinking more than you need can lead to "exercise-associated hyponatremia", or EAH. This is an imbalance in the level of electrolytes in your blood, caused by drinking more liquid than your kidneys can excrete.

One way of knowing how hydrated you are is to examine the colour of your urine after a run (see box, below left), ensuring you know the correct amount of water you need to drink during each training session.

ARE YOU DEHYDRATED?

The easiest way to check whether you are dehydrated is to collect a sample of your urine in a transparent glass and examine its colour. Ideally, your urine will be one of the first three colours shown in the chart. If it is any darker, you should rehydrate as soon as possible.

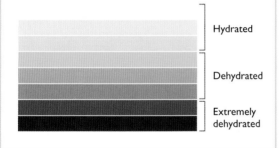

Hydrated

Dehydrated

Extremely dehydrated

FLUID GAIN AND LOSS

The human body takes in and excretes water in various different ways. The average percentages of fluid gain and loss are shown in the diagram below.

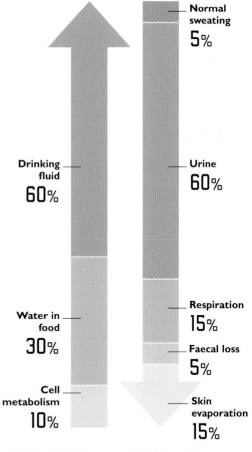

Normal sweating **5%**

Drinking fluid **60%**

Urine **60%**

Water in food **30%**

Respiration **15%**

Faecal loss **5%**

Cell metabolism **10%**

Skin evaporation **15%**

WATER INTAKE
Your body gains fluid from three sources: drinks, the water found in food, and "metabolic water" – fluid that is released when you burn carbohydrates and fats.

WATER LOSS
You lose water in five main ways, though your fluid loss will vary depending on the air humidity and temperature, and the intensity and duration of your training session.

SLOW THE AGEING PROCESS

Ageing is something that affects us all, but there are certain things you can do to slow the process. Starting a running, stretching, and resistance training programme alongside a healthy eating plan can help to stave off the effects of ageing. In addition, keeping stress levels at bay and protecting yourself from the sun can do wonders for promoting a youthful appearance. In mature women, this regimen can delay or reduce some of the symptoms of menopause.

Exercise to stay young

Staying physically active delays the signs of ageing in many ways. In addition to lifting your mood and boosting energy levels, running regularly can improve your ability to use oxygen. Running slows the deterioration of your VO2 max – the maximum amount of oxygen your body can obtain and use during intense exercise (see p112). The more oxygen your lungs can take in, the more oxygen your body can use efficiently. This increased efficiency can slow the signs of ageing.

Simply put, oxygenated cells live longer, and this applies to those that make up your skin, your muscles, and even your brain. So, as a runner, you can look forward to a prolonged youthful complexion and musculature, and mental sharpness. The high impact of running also strengthens your bones to delay the onset of osteoporosis (particularly in women), and the earlier you start, the stronger your bones will be. Losing lean muscle mass as you age is a fact of life,

A balanced diet: drink plenty of milk since it contains a range of vitamins and minerals, such as calcium, which is thought to slow the effects of osteoporosis.

and unfortunately, muscle mass is a factor in determining your metabolic rate, or the rate at which you use calories. Supplementing your running with resistance exercises (see pp52–59) can slow the rate of muscular atrophy and prevent weight gain associated with the ageing process. Stretching regularly (see pp42–49) will keep you feeling limber into old age.

WHY WEAR SUNSCREEN?

The ultraviolet (UV) rays of the sun are ever-present, even on cloudy days, and they are extremely hazardous to your skin. UV rays steal moisture from your skin and slow the rate of cellular turnover, which leads to premature ageing in the form of wrinkles and discolouration. UV rays can also cause skin cancer, so always wear a sport-ready sunscreen of at least SPF 15 for adequate protection.

Fight ageing with a total fitness regimen: running, stretching, and resistance training, in conjunction with a healthy lifestyle, can help slow many of the signs of ageing.

Diet and stress levels

Exercise is not the only factor that matters in an anti-ageing regimen. It is just as important to eat a balanced diet, rich in a variety of healthy foods. Fruits and vegetables provide the body with vital nutrients, including antioxidants such as beta-carotene, selenium, and vitamins A, C, and E, which appear to protect cells from destructive molecules called free radicals. To help maintain strong bones, women should take daily calcium supplements or consume two to three servings of dairy products such as yogurt or milk every day.

Keeping stress levels under control is yet another way to delay the signs of ageing. Stress causes the body to release hormones such as adrenaline and cortisol into the bloodstream. Both have been linked to premature ageing, so try as often as you can to keep life's lesser disasters in perspective.

RUNNING FOR WEIGHT LOSS

Starting a running regimen is one of the best things you can do to lose weight. It burns more calories than almost any other form of exercise, and it tones your lower body without bulking up muscles. However, running on its own will probably not yield optimum weight loss results. You must also modify your diet and be mindful of the number and quality of calories you consume. Read the following section for information and advice on how to shed weight safely and effectively.

Calories do count

Forget what you've heard about fad diets. The truth is that calories do count, and the only way to lose weight is to burn off more than you consume. A safe amount to weight to lose is 0.5kg (1 pound) per week. Since there are approximately 3,500 calories in 0.5kg (1 pound), to lose this weight, you have to create a 3,500-calorie deficit over the course of a week. However, if speedy weight loss is not your goal, bear in mind that any deficit at all will cause you to lose some weight. Even if you don't change your diet and add running to your life, you will lose some weight. The best and healthiest way to lose weight steadily, however, is through a combination of diet and exercise.

Modify your diet

You must be mindful of how many calories you consume normally, and then make restrictions and substitutions where necessary. To do this, record your daily diet for one week, and then estimate

Run for a slim physique: for shedding excess weight, running, in conjunction with a calorie-controlled diet, is a winning combination.

your calorie intake per day from this data. You can then see where cuts and substitutions can be made. For example, replace high-calorie snacks with fruit, eat fish where you used to eat red meat, and switch to skimmed milk from whole milk. You will be astonished to see how small changes like these in your diet will yield rapid results. For more substitutions, consult the chart (see *right*).

That said, you should never eat fewer than 1,200 calories per day, especially if you are running regularly. This level of severe calorie restriction can cause you to lose weight too rapidly, and you may lose metabolically active muscle instead of fat. This can slow your base metabolism in the long term, which can lead to future weight gain.

A numbers game

Running is a great way to fine-tune your calorie intake and output, since it burns roughly 100 calories per 1.6km (1 mile) if you are training at RPE level six, or at 60 per cent of your MHR. So, if you run four days a week, for 4.8km (3 miles) per session, you will burn approximately 1,200 extra calories that week. If you wish to burn even more than that, add another 4.8-km (3-mile) run and you'll burn 1,500 calories over the course of the week. You can run less than this, and eat fewer calories instead, or you can increase your running and eat a little more.

Your body will actually burn calories at a faster rate *after* your run as well. Running revs up your metabolism, and it stays humming well beyond the duration of your run. In essence, you will be burning calories at an elevated rate for up to 12 hours after your run.

Running builds muscle in your legs, and since muscle tissue is metabolically active, the more of it you have, the higher your resting metabolism will be. So, even on a rest day, you will burn more calories than you did before you started your running regimen.

SUBSTITUTIONS FOR SAVING CALORIES

Try	Instead of	Calories saved
Frozen yogurt (170)	Ice cream (240)	70
Banana (93)	Banana bread (338)	245
Diet cola (0)	Regular cola (150)	150
Nonfat yogurt (30)	Crème fraîche (62)	32
Pumpkin seeds (36)	Peanuts (105)	69
Raisins (60)	Chocolate (250)	190
Skimmed milk (86)	Whole milk (150)	114

all comparative portion sizes are equal

A word about high-protein diets

You may be familiar with some high-protein, low-cabohydrate diets that are popular at the moment. They may induce weight loss, but are they are not necessarily healthy or sustainable, particularly if you intend to embark on a running programme. I have found from personal experience that my energy levels are much lower on these types of diets. High-protein diets that exclude carbohydrates can put a strain on your kidneys and other internal organs, which could possibly be harmful in the long term, particularly for those with a pre-existing kidney condition.

In addition, if your body is unable to get an adequate amount of energy because of a reduced carbohydrate intake, you will not be able to run efficiently. Indeed, any diet which cuts out one food group in favour of another has risks; the body requires a balanced nutritional intake in order to perform at its best (see pp72–75). It is healthier to eat a variety of foods in moderation, and use running to burn off any excess calories you consume.

WEIGHT-LOSS PROGRAMME

Running burns calories faster than almost any other form of exercise – at 100 calories per 1.6km (1 mile), it is a wonderful way to lose weight. Before you begin your weight-loss programme, you must first determine your average daily calorie intake. To lose about 0.5kg (1 pound) per week, you will need to reduce this number by 500 calories per day though a combination of dietary changes and exercise.

So, for example, if you typically consume 2,000 calories per day and you then begin to run 1.6km (1 mile) each day, you will burn 100 calories daily through exercise. You will therefore only need to eliminate 400 calories from your diet (consuming 1,600 calories) in order to achieve your 500-calorie deficit. On non-running days, you should limit your dietary intake to 1,500 calories, reducing your food intake by the full 500 calories to stay on track. This deficit of about 500 calories per day will result in a total weight loss of 0.5kg (1 pound) over seven days.

The beauty of this weight-loss programme lies in its flexibility and simplicity. If you miss a scheduled run, scale back your food intake, or if you have a special dinner to attend, add an extra run to your week. There are no special or forbidden foods on this programme: there's just a simple mathematical formula and your common sense!

For weight loss, all runs should be done at conversational pace. The eight-week programme on the right should result in a total weight loss of roughly 4kg (8lbs).

	Rest days
	Run days

	Day 1	Day 2
WEEK 1	Jog 1.6km (1 mile) Eat 400 fewer calories	Rest day Eat 500 fewer calories
WEEK 2	**Day 8** Rest day Eat 500 fewer calories	**Day 9** Jog 1.6km (1 mile) Eat 400 fewer calories
WEEK 3	**Day 15** Jog 3.2km (2 miles) Eat 300 fewer calories	**Day 16** Rest day Eat 500 fewer calories
WEEK 4	**Day 22** Jog 4.8km (3 miles) Eat 200 fewer calories	**Day 23** Rest day Eat 500 fewer calories
WEEK 5	**Day 29** Jog 3.2km (2 miles) Eat 300 fewer calories	**Day 30** Rest day Eat 500 fewer calories
WEEK 6	**Day 36** Jog 4.8km (3 miles) Eat 200 fewer calories	**Day 37** Rest day Eat 500 fewer calories
WEEK 7	**Day 43** Jog 4.8km (3 miles) Eat 200 fewer calories	**Day 44** Rest day Eat 500 fewer calories
WEEK 8	**Day 50** Jog 6.4km (4 miles) Eat 100 fewer calories	**Day 51** Rest day Eat 500 fewer calories

Day 3	Day 4	Day 5	Day 6	Day 7	Total
Jog 1.6km (1 mile) Eat 400 fewer calories	Rest day Eat 500 fewer calories	Jog 1.6km (1 mile) Eat 400 fewer calories	Rest day Eat 500 fewer calories	Jog 1.6km (1 mile) Eat 400 fewer calories	−3,500 calories

Day 10	Day 11	Day 12	Day 13	Day 14	Total
Jog 1.6km (1 mile) Eat 400 fewer calories	Rest day Eat 500 fewer calories	Jog 1.6km (1 mile) Eat 400 fewer calories	Jog 1.6km (1 mile) Eat 400 fewer calories	Rest day Eat 500 fewer calories	−3,500 calories

Day 17	Day 18	Day 19	Day 20	Day 21	Total
Jog 3.2km (2 miles) Eat 300 fewer calories	Rest day Eat 500 fewer calories	Jog 3.2km (2 miles) Eat 300 fewer calories	Jog 3.2km (2 miles) Eat 300 fewer calories	Rest day Eat 500 fewer calories	−3,500 calories

Day 24	Day 25	Day 26	Day 27	Day 28	Total
Jog 3.2km (2 miles) Eat 300 fewer calories	Rest day Eat 500 fewer calories	Jog 4.8km (3 miles) Eat 200 fewer calories	Rest day Eat 500 fewer calories	Jog 4.8km (3 miles) Eat 200 fewer calories	−3,500 calories

Day 31	Day 32	Day 33	Day 34	Day 35	Total
Jog 4.8km (3 miles) Eat 200 fewer calories	Rest day Eat 500 fewer calories	Jog 4.8km (3 miles) Eat 200 fewer calories	Jog 4.8km (3 miles) Eat 200 fewer calories	Rest day Eat 500 fewer calories	−3,500 calories

Day 38	Day 39	Day 40	Day 41	Day 42	Total
Jog 3.2km (2 miles) Eat 300 fewer calories	Rest day Eat 500 fewer calories	Jog 4.8km (3 miles) Eat 200 fewer calories	Rest day Eat 500 fewer calories	Jog 4.8km (3 miles) Eat 200 fewer calories	−3,500 calories

Day 45	Day 46	Day 47	Day 48	Day 49	Total
Jog 4.8km (3 miles) Eat 200 fewer calories	Rest day Eat 500 fewer calories	Jog 3.2km (2 miles) Eat 300 fewer calories	Jog 4.8km (3 miles) Eat 200 fewer calories	Rest day Eat 500 fewer calories	−3,500 calories

Day 52	Day 53	Day 54	Day 55	Day 56	Total
Jog 6.4km (4 miles) Eat 100 fewer calories	Rest day Eat 500 fewer calories	Jog 4.8km (3 miles) Eat 200 fewer calories	Rest day Eat 500 fewer calories	Jog 6.4km (4 miles) Eat 100 fewer calories	−3,500 calories

INTERMEDIATE LEVEL AND BEYOND

MY FIRST RUNNING MEMORY IS OF BEING NINE YEARS OLD ON THE PLAYGROUND DURING A GAME OF TAG. MY GOAL WAS TO BE THAT LAST PERSON TAGGED. AS I RAN, I IMAGINED MYSELF FLOWING AWAY FROM THE OTHER KIDS, SEEING THE GAP BETWEEN ME AND MY PURSUERS WIDENING AS I HEADED FOR THE OUTER SPACE OF THE PLAYGROUND. I FELT AS IF I WERE FLOATING, RELAXED AND FREE. TODAY, WHEN I FEEL MYSELF GETTING TIGHT ON A RUN, I RETURN TO THIS SAME MENTAL IMAGE, FEELING MYSELF FLOWING ACROSS THE GROUND, WORRYING ONLY ABOUT NOT GETTING TAGGED.

TECHNIQUE

You were born with your own unique running style, whether you are new to the sport, or a veteran runner. Think of it as a puzzle you are trying to piece together. Regardless of your footstrike, stride, posture, or arm position, your form should come naturally, and feel comfortable above all else. As a child running across a playground, your body knew instinctively how to run – it's just a matter of reacquainting yourself with this long-forgotten natural running style.

Styles vary – even among Olympians

People tell me that I have good running form. However, running form varies from person to person, and I believe that there is no one style that runners must conform to in order to excel. Karel Lismont, a European champion and Olympic marathon medallist from Belgium, shuffled along with his head tilted severely to the right. Kenny Moore, a superb writer and Olympic runner, once described the style of another marathon runner from the former Soviet Union as "stomping on ants". This all goes to show that there's room for excellence no matter what your running style or form.

Relax and regain your natural style

Using a mental image from my childhood, in which I was running across a playground during a game of tag, helps me to relax and regain my natural form. This type of visualization can do the same for you. Simply let go of yourself in your present activity, running for speed and aiming for good technique. Imagine yourself, instead, as a child, running carefree across a field, and your natural, relaxed running style will emerge.

Arm position

The rhythm and position of your arms helps to both propel your body forwards and stabilize your balance, but there is no correct way to do it. Some people bend their arms and "pump" them back and

You were born with your own unique running style: you did not think of your form as a child running across the playground, and you shouldn't think about it now, either.

forth while running. Other runners keep their arms fairly straight, holding them static. The most important thing about your natural arm position and rhythm is that it complements your inherent running form. Let your body tell you what feels most natural, instead of trying to control the movement intellectually. Try the following exercise (see *opposite*) to find your ideal arm position.

Arm position

To find your natural arm position, your entire body should be in running motion. This will prevent your mind from controlling the movement, allowing your arms to go where they "want" to go. Your body will instinctively synchronize your arm motion with that of your legs.

arms
relaxed

let arms
rise up

1 Start running at your natural and easy conversational pace. Clear your head as you let your arms dangle by your sides.

2 Let your arms rise up to a comfortable position, and allow them to swing in a natural rhythm. Do not think about where you are going to place them – simply let them join in with the overall motion of your body.

Body posture

Many runners worry too much about their body posture. Do what comes naturally as you run, and you'll be doing what's right for you. If you try too hard to change your natural running posture, your unique style will fall out of sync, which can contribute to discomfort and possibly injury. Simply stay relaxed and visualize yourself running across the playground as a child, and your natural posture will emerge. One caveat: your body angle will necessarily change slightly when you run on hills (see below), and you should not fight this shift. In running, your body's instincts are nearly always right, so you should trust them.

Footstrike

You are either a either toe-striker or heel-striker, based on the way your foot plants on the ground and pushes itself off. Footstrike is related to running posture and is part of your inherited biomechanics, so you should not try to change it. Regardless of footstrike, you should always aim to land gently on the ground to minimize the shock absorbed by your body from impact.

Most runners are heel-strikers, which means they land on their heel first, roll through their foot, and then push off the ground with their toes. Toe-strikers land on the ball of their foot, rolling back to their heel as they push off the ground. There is no one footstrike that is right for everyone – the footstrike that comes naturally is the one that is best for you. Neither one yields faster times or fewer injuries than the other. It really only affects what type of shoe you buy: heel-strikers need shoes with reinforced heel counters (see pp22–23).

Footstrike and posture connection

Your torso is your centre of gravity, or the point around which your body balances itself. Since your body naturally positions its centre of gravity right over

As you can see from this picture, I am a toe-striker: this means that I plant my foot toe first. It also means that I lean forwards a little bit, too.

the point where your foot plants, your natural running posture and footstrike influence one another. If you heel-strike, you will probably run with moderately erect posture, and if you toe-strike, you will probably lean forwards slightly.

These pairings of posture and footstrike help the body to balance itself. Stick with your natural pairing, since changing one aspect of your form may interfere with another. One exception to the rule is when running uphill: in this situation, most runners lean forwards and toe-strike. Leaning into a hill assists runners with their climb.

POSTURE AND FOOTSTRIKE

This runner is a toe-striker. She leans forwards slightly
when running so that her torso, or centre of gravity,
is directly above where her foot plants.

Forward-leaning posture
allows her centre of gravity
to be directly above where
her foot plants on the ground.

Toe-strikers
land on the ball of the foot and
then roll back to the heel as they
push off the ground.

POSTURE AND FOOTSTRIKE

This runner is a heel-striker. She leans back slightly when running so that her torso, or centre of gravity, is directly above where her heel plants.

Upright posture
allows her centre of gravity to be directly above where her heel plants on the ground.

Heel-strikers
land on the heel of the foot and then roll through the foot to push off the ground.

Body type and running style

Your body shape and size affect your running, but if you learn which type you are and work with your strengths, it doesn't have to slow you down. There are three main body types: ectomorph, mesomorph, and endomorph. Ectomorphs are marked by a thin, long build. They tend to have small, light frames, and difficulty building muscle. Mesomorphs are more muscular in build than ectomorphs, and their bones are heavier and broader than those of the ectomorph as well.

Endomorphs are a bit softer and fuller-figured than both ectomorphs and endomorphs, but their skeletal structure in both length and breadth resembles that of the mesomorph. Bear in mind, however, that most people are a combination of these types rather than an extreme version of one. Many people actually lie somewhere between an endomorph and a mesomorph in build.

Any body can excel

I am willing to admit that if you want to run in an Olympic marathon, it is best to be relatively small and thin. However, this is not a prerequisite for excellence. In fact, I have always thought that the more unlikely one's body type might appear for running, the greater the potential psychological advantage in competition. But more importantly, great running is down to training, not body type.

Joan Benoit Samuelson, the winner of the first women's Olympic marathon, is an exceptional athlete and a fierce and extremely savvy competitor. Her body type is not that of the stereotypical runner – she is relatively muscular and short in stature. Great Britain's Paula Radcliffe, by contrast, is tall and lanky. In fact, she is one of the tallest women marathon runners in history. Both of these women, regardless of their perceived physical limitations, reached the pinnacle of achievement in long-distance running.

Breaking the mould: unusual body types, like Paula Radcliffe's tall frame, are no impediment to running success.

Nurture, not nature

Marathon success derives from training rather than body type or culture, with competitors of many nationalities winning medals over the years. For a while, many of the men's Olympic marathon medals went to runners with East Asian body types. This is a stark contrast to the wispy forms of the East African men and women who have won recent Olympic marathons. This shows that innovative training, rather than inherited physical traits, wins gold medals.

Stride length versus turnover

Turnover and stride are the two main factors that determine the pace of your running. Stride length is the length of each step you take when running, and turnover is the number of steps you take over a set distance. Everyone has a natural stride length and turnover, and as usual, what feels comfortable is probably best and most efficient for you.

Stride length, or gait, receives all too much attention, and the misconceptions surrounding it can lead to injury. For example, in some instances beginning runners overstride, taking unnaturally long steps. They are often consciously trying to cover as much ground as possible with each step. Try not to fall into this trap. This unnatural extension of stride length may interfere with your natural running form, which can cause muscular strain and injury.

In the beginning, if you think about stride at all, you may be thinking about it too much. If you wish to improve your pace, concentrate instead on increasing your turnover and try to stay relaxed. This quicker turnover will allow you to maintain your relaxed, natural form, which in turn will help you to land as softly as possible. This does not

LONG AND SHORT STRIDE

Stride length varies from runner to runner, but it's usually an extension of your height and build. Tall runners tend to have long strides, while short runners have shorter ones. If you are tall and want to increase your speed, gradually lengthen your stride length. If you are a short runner, however, you should focus on your power, and increase turnover (*see opposite*).

Long stride
If you have a long and lean physique, aim to increase your pace by lengthening your normal stride length. Don't overstretch yourself, though, since this can lead to strain-induced injury.

Short stride
If you are physically short and powerful, quicken your rate of turnover, or the number of steps you take over a set distance. Concentrate on your strength, which is muscular power.

mean you should *try* to land softly. To be light on your feet and land softly, simply stay relaxed as you increase your turnover. This will help speed muscular recovery time.

Work on your strengths

Don't worry about the body type you were given. Aim instead to do the best with what you have, focusing on that which you can control through training. You can improve your speed either by gradually increasing stride length or by increasing turnover. However, depending on your body type and level of training, it is safest to focus on increasing one or the other, rather than both.

Different body types run differently, but equally well. You simply need to find your strength and work with it. If you are a tall and lean ectomorph with powerful strides, like Paula Radcliffe, concentrate on lengthening your stride gradually and in a relaxed manner; if you are short and muscular (mesomorph or endomorph) with a shuffling stride, like Joan Benoit Samuelson, increase your turnover, taking quicker strides.

TURNOVER

The two runners below have two different body types and two different strengths. The ectomorph on top works on her stride length, subtly lengthening her stride, while the mesomorph below works on increasing her turnover, taking rapid strides. They both cover the same distance between two trees in exactly the same amount of time. Neither is superior.

Tall and lean
This runner has a powerful stride. Over a set distance, she subtly lengthens her stride, taking six long strides.

Small and muscular
This runner increases her turnover. Over the same set distance as above, she takes seven rapid strides.

Training pace

Your pace, or speed, is determined not only by your cardiovascular fitness but also by the length of your stride and the rate of your turnover, or the number of strides you take over a given distance. Your training pace must be that which is most comfortable and natural for you, and it must be done at conversational pace.

Your training pace is the average number of minutes it takes you to run 1.6km (1 mile). Your optimal training pace should allow you to run at conversational pace throughout your workout, so don't use a hard anaerobic run (that includes hill training or interval training) when trying to work out your average pace.

To determine your training pace, devise a course that is the same distance you would cover on a typical run. If you normally run a loop that you think is 8km (5 miles), map out a course of the same length to minimize your margin of error. Run this course at conversational pace and time yourself for the duration of your run, or record yourself with a fitness tracker. Try not to run any faster than you would normally, since this may skew your data. Divide your time by 8 (or 5 for miles) to get your average training pace. So, if it takes you 50 minutes, your pace should be a 6:15-minute kilometre (10-minute mile).

Racing pace

Your racing pace may be slightly faster than your training pace. A good rule of thumb is to race at a pace that is one minute per 1.6km (1 mile) faster than your training pace. So, if you run a 6:15-minute kilometre (10-minute mile) in training, in a race, aim to run 5:40-minute kilometres (9-minute miles). That said, first time marathon runners should race at their training pace – just finishing the event is enough.

Hitting your goal race pace is a matter of subtlety: slightly increase your stride length *and* your speed of turnover, both by no more than 10 per cent. Increasing your stride length and turnover by this small amount will improve your pace as much as you can; this increase should be safe and sustainable during a race. Any more than this will feel unnatural and could lead to burnout or injury.

SAMPLE TRAINING TO RACING PACE CHARTS

Your race pace should be no more than one minute per 1.6km (1 mile) faster than your training pace to avoid injury and muscular strain. See the sample charts below to get acquainted with this subtle increase in speed. The chart on the left uses kilometres, while the one on the right uses miles. Times are rounded to the nearest minute.

Distance	TRAINING PACE	RACING PACE
	6:15-minute km	5:40-minute km
1.6km	10 min	9 min
5km	31 min	28 min
8km	50 min	45 min
10km	1 hr 2 min	56 min
21km	2 hr 11 min	1 hr 58 min
42.1km	4 hr 22 min	3 hr 56 min

Distance	TRAINING PACE	RACING PACE
	10-minute mile	9-minute mile
1 mile	10 min	9 min
3.1 miles	31 min	28 min
5 miles	50 min	45 min
6.2 miles	1 hr 2 min	56 min
13.1 miles	2 hr 11 min	1 hr 58 min
26.2 miles	4 hr 22 min	3 hr 56 min

NB: 6:15-minute kilometre = 10-minute mile; 5:40-minute kilometre = 9-minute mile

Training pace to racing pace

Your training pace is the speed at which you routinely run. It should be feel comfortable and natural. Your racing pace, unlike your training routine, is a one-time thing. Race up to one minute per 1.6km (1 mile) faster than you train, but the trick is to *subtly* increase your stride length and turnover.

comfortable stride

increased stride length

Training pace should be conversational (RPE level six, *see pp26–27*), and your body should feel comfortable. Stride length and turnover should feel natural and never overstretched. Use your training pace as a base by which to determine your race pace.

For racing pace, increase stride length and turnover by as much as 10 per cent, but you should never feel as though you are straining. Your RPE can go up to level seven. This will yield a racing pace of up to one minute per 1.6km (1 mile) faster than your training pace.

INJURY AND OVERUSE

Running is a good way to find your orthopaedic (skeletal) weak spots. However, I have always viewed these aches and pains as indications of when and how much to ease off my training. The physically stressful pounding and repetitive motion of running forces the body to send signals when it needs a bit more healing time in a particular area which, in the long term, can help prevent chronic injury.

Technique and injury

Injury is not a result of "good" or "bad" running technique. It is instead the body's weaknesses showing through from time to time. These can be aggravated by a range of things, including overtraining, running fast downhill or on surfaces that are too hard, and not varying your route enough. Watch out for slight pain, which is an early sign of injury, and always switch to alternate training when necessary.

Watch your footing

Many injuries are just a result of bad luck, so always be mindful of your footing. Look out for cracks in the pavement, exposed tree roots, and abnormalities in the road, since all of these can trip you up and cause serious injury. Mis-stepping or losing your footing is the main cause of a sprained ankle (for preventative exercise, see p105).

You should also avoid running fast downhill. It can be the prelude to an orthopaedic nightmare, and it offers very little in the way of cardiovascular benefit. It may feel good at the time, with the wind in your hair, but with each step, you are falling just that much further and with just that much more speed; the impact is much greater going downhill than it is when running on the flat or uphill. Both muscles and joints suffer heavily from downhill running, and those predisposed to back problems put themselves at high risk.

Bone and cartilage injuries

It is difficult to determine whether pain is caused by trauma to soft tissue (muscle or tendon) or to bone or cartilage. The latter is a more serious condition, requiring immediate rest and medical attention. A good rule of thumb is to assume it is cartilage- or bone-related injury if pain is severe and accompanied by swelling and/or bruising. If pain is constant and persistent from the start of your run, or if it centres around a joint (including the knee, ankle, hip, or toe), you should stop running immediately and see a doctor. You may be unable to run for up to six weeks. Running on this type of injury could cause permanent damage to your body (for more on fractures, see box, p98).

Muscular injury

While less serious than a bone injury, muscular strain can be very painful, requiring up to six weeks of rest as well. Do not hobble along on an injury: you are not likely to achieve any cardiovascular benefits. In fact, your altered form could even cause injury somewhere else.

If you feel a slight strain (not pain) in your body, act early to prevent full-blown injury. Scale back your running and supplement your routine with low-impact forms of training, such as swimming or cycling. In addition, practise the following stretching and strengthening exercises (see pp99–107) to prevent injury.

FLAT AND EVEN FOR SAFETY
Running on a flat, level surface that absorbs
much of the shock of impact, such as a track,
minimizes the incidence of injury.

INJURY PREVENTION

Running-induced injuries can occur in a variety of areas, but they most commonly affect the feet, ankles, shins, knees, back, and hips. These are usually due to damage to bone and cartilage, or to soft tissue or muscle. That said, if you know where your own most vulnerable areas are, there are some preventative measures you can take. Listen to your body when little aches and pains strike, and use the following tips and exercises to prevent full-blown injury.

Shin splints: causes and symptoms

A common overuse injury in runners, "shin splints" is an all-inclusive term for pain shooting up and down the front of the lower leg. Researchers are not sure of the exact cause of shin splints, but many experts believe they result from a sharp increase in a runner's typical weekly distance or intensity.

In young runners, shin splints can be due to tiny hairline stress fractures down the front of the shin bone, while in mature runners pain is sometimes due to the sheath surrounding the shin muscles becoming detached from the shin bone.

Shin splints: prevention and correction

To prevent shin splints from happening in the first place, avoid abruptly increasing the distance or intensity of your runs, and stretch your shins regularly (see *opposite*). If hairline fractures in your shin bone are causing shin splints, rest and seek medical attention immediately. Six weeks of total rest from running and other high-impact sports is recommended in order to allow your bones to heal.

In the case of soft tissue problems such as muscular inflammation, or if the sheath becomes detached from the bone, care for your shins with ice, massage, and rest. Massage your shins with ice wrapped in cloth, then stop, let the shins warm up, and repeat. This helps reduce inflammation in sore soft tissue and speeds up circulation for healing: it will also allow the sheath to reattach to the bone.

FRACTURES AND HOT SPOTS

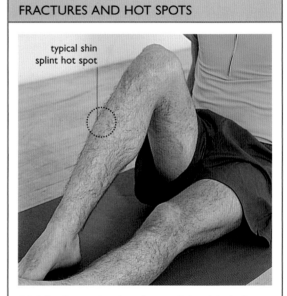

typical shin splint hot spot

A hairline fracture is a tiny, microscopic break in the bone and, if you get one, it can prevent you from running for up to six weeks. Fortunately, a fracture gives a warning sign in the form of a "hot spot." It is called this because the point at which the fracture is set to occur usually feels hot, sore, and tender to the touch.

The pain can come and go at first, but it eventually becomes constant. Immediately rest a hot spot and avoid running in favour of some form of non-impact aerobic activity for at least two weeks. The area may heal up enough to let you start running again. If you run on a hot spot, you risk a full-blown fracture and long-term layoff. Instead of being incapacitated for two weeks, you would be unable to run for a much longer six weeks.

Shin splint prevention stretch

This exercise can help prevent shin splints by stretching and relaxing tight shin muscles. You should aim to perform this stretch every day if you have recently increased your run's distance or intensity. If you feel a hot spot (*see box, opposite*), you may have a hairline fracture, so rest and see a doctor immediately.

1 Sit on your knees on a soft surface, such as a carpet or mat, with your hands on your thighs. Your feet should be on either side of your body with the fronts of your shins flat on the mat.

2 Sit back between your heels and hold this position for 10–15 seconds, then relax. Repeat 3–5 times.

rest hands on thighs

buttocks between feet

feel it here

KNEE INJURY

When I was young, I thought my knees were indestructible. They looked solid and durable: I have big, out-of-proportion knee caps, and I never had any knee trouble until I turned 50 and the cartilage in my right knee simply wore out. Of course, by then I had run a huge distance, and just as running shoes have a finite lifespan, so do your knees. However, by using the preventative exercises and palliative tips below, you can prolong the health of your knees.

Causes and symptoms

Injury to the knee is very common, and most runners will develop some sort of knee discomfort at some stage during their running years. The most prevalent type of knee injury is caused by weak or worn-down cartilage behind the knee cap. This cartilage acts as a buffer between bone rubbing against bone and, when it has worn away completely, as it did with me, severe pain ensues. The pad of cartilage behind my right knee was almost worn down to nothing.

Knee pain can also occur when the cartilage that holds the knee steady becomes strained, torn, or displaced. This causes significant pain and interferes with comfortable movement because the knee is no longer held stable.

Pain on the outside of the knee may be caused by a condition known as iliotibial band syndrome (ITBS), which is a lack of strength or flexibility in the iliotibial band. This muscle runs down the outside of the thigh and attaches to the lateral side of the tibia bone, which is just below the knee. It helps to stabilize the knee when running, but friction (caused by the running motion) may cause the iliotibial band to become irritated and painful.

Prevention and correction

Most recreational runners don't clock the same distances as the elite athlete, and so are less likely to wear away all of their cartilage. Even so, it is

WHAT ABOUT KNEE BRACES?

For alleviating knee pain knee braces, also known as supports, can sometimes be useful. There are several different types of knee brace available, but most of them work by protecting or supporting the knee, or by limiting painful knee movement.

Generally speaking, knee braces tend to be most effective when worn after an injury has occurred, particularly in the front of the knee, but some athletes wear them as a preventative measure. You can buy simple braces from a chemist or more specialized models from your doctor. If your knee pain lasts longer than a week, however, you should seek medical advice.

wise to take as many precautions as possible to delay any deterioration. To help prevent the onset of knee pain, use exercises, such as the following (see *opposite*), to strengthen the muscles that stabilize the knee. In addition, wearing a knee brace, which you can buy from any high-quality sports shop, can also stabilize the knee and minimize pain while running. In extreme and chronic instances, corrective surgery may be needed, so consult your physician. Fortunately, certain types of knee surgery are relatively routine.

If you have ITBS, the following exercise may be too painful to perform. Run less frequently than you would normally, stretch (see *pp44–46*), and regularly place ice wrapped in cloth on your knee instead.

Knee injury prevention exercise

The key to preventing knee injury is strengthening the muscles that hold the knee in place. This will minimize abnormal movement of the knee cap, while also cushioning it from impact. This exercise may not be appropriate for those suffering from ITBS, which is marked by pain on the outside of the knee.

1 Sit upright on a bench or chair, holding the underside of your seat for balance. Lift your right leg slowly until it reaches a right angle from your body.

2 Hold your leg in this position for 10–30 seconds, or until you feel a burn in the muscle surrounding the knee, then relax. Switch legs and repeat 3–5 times on each leg.

keep back straight

leg at 90° angle

BACK AND HIP PAIN

Many runners experience back pain that can result from any number of things, from skeletal problems to trapped nerves to muscular tension. Back and hip pain, both common conditions, are often related to one another. Tightness in the piriformis muscle can cause pain in the lower back, as can compressed vertebrae, which are a chain of bones that comprise the spine. However, if back pain is severe, seek medical attention.

Causes and symptoms

Muscular strain is the most common, and least serious, cause of back pain. The impact of the pounding motion of running can increase tension in the lower back, which can cause discomfort. One of the most common sources of lower back pain is piriformis syndrome, which is actually caused by the piriformis muscle in your buttock. The repetitive motion of running can cause extreme tightness in the hips, which can lead to the inflammation of the piriformis muscle. This swollen muscle can then put pressure on the sciatic nerve, which passes down through the buttocks and further down the legs. This leads to discomfort in the lower back, hip, buttock, and down one leg.

Another cause of back pain, also a result of an "impinged" or pinched nerve, is not muscular in origin, but skeletal. The pounding motion of running can cause the small cushions in the spine, called discs, to compress. As with piriformis syndrome, this condition can pinch the spinal nerve roots, which in turn causes spasms of pain.

To predict a pinched back nerve, have a friend help you check the strength of your big toe. Sit down on the ground and extend your legs in front of you. While your heel is on the ground, have your friend hold on to your big toe. Try to resist them as they gently bend it down and away from you. If the toe is weak or collapses forwards, it may mean you have a trapped nerve.

CHECK YOUR POSTURE

Back pain can also result from poor posture. A tendency to lean on one leg, slouch while standing or seated, or over-arch your back can contribute to tense muscles and put undue stress on the back. Everyone's body is different, so good posture varies from person to person. In all cases, however, the spine should form a slight S-shape (when viewed from the side). To practise good posture, imagine lengthening the space between each vertebra in your spine. Standing tall can help reduce pressure on the muscles and bones in the back. Pilates and the Alexander technique are also thought to help improve posture.

Prevention and correction

Relaxation is the key to relieving most back pain. In the case of piriformis syndrome, try the piriformis stretch (see opposite, top). This will relax and lengthen the piriformis muscle in the buttock and reduce the inflammation, thereby relieving pressure on the sciatic nerve.

The back relaxer (see opposite, bottom) can also help alleviate pain associated with compressed vertebrae, since the muscles surrounding the trapped nerve tend to tense up, causing sharp pain. Visualize the muscles of your lower back relaxing and the vertebrae of your spine lengthening as you stretch your lower back and press your spine into the ground beneath you. If pain persists, however, contact your doctor.

Piriformis stretch

If you are prone to an aching lower back, your piriformis may be the culprit. Perform this gentle stretch every day to loosen tightness in this muscle, which is located deep in the buttock, and to relax the lower back. To avoid exacerbating pain, take care not to use too much force when performing this stretch.

pull calf across body

Lie on your back on a mat or carpet. Bend your right knee and place your left hand on your calf. Gently pull your calf across your body, feeling the stretch in your hip and buttock. Hold this position for 10–30 seconds, then rest. Switch legs and repeat 3–5 times.

Back relaxer

A tight, tense lower back can lead to pain, marked by spasms or a dull ache. Many people who suffer from back pain find that mental tricks can be helpful when done in conjunction with gentle exercises, such as the following. As you perform this stretch, try to visualize the tension in your back melting away.

hold leg just below knee

Lie on your back on a mat or carpet. Bend your right knee to your chest. Use both hands to pull your leg towards your body, holding it just below your knee. Let your back relax and sink into the floor for 10–30 seconds, then relax. Switch legs and repeat 3–5 times.

FOOT AND ANKLE INJURY

Be kind to your feet, since you are asking them to perform for you. Arch, ankle, toenail, and fungal problems can all take their toll, so be pro-active about preventing these conditions from inhibiting your running programme in the first place. For healthy feet, practise the preventative measures on pages 104–107. For further help in finding the best shoe for your foot shape and size, consult pages 20–23.

Causes and symptoms

The most common foot and ankle problems associated with running include sprained ankles, blisters, ingrown toenails, arch soreness, bunions, and fungal problems. However, with a little care, most of these conditions can be easily prevented.

Prevention and correction

A sprained ankle most often results from a mis-step on uneven terrain or from weak ankles, which can be corrected with strengthening exercises opposite.

Blisters are caused by chafing from ill-fitting footwear, while burning fungus often results from damp socks or shoes. Ingrown toenails, a painful condition in which the sides of the nail actually grow into the skin, stem from overzealous nail-cutting using poor technique. Bunions, which are hereditary extra bone growths on the foot, may be aggravated by tight shoes. And finally, arch pain is most commonly caused by high arches that are weak and collapsing. Try the preventative exercises opposite to strengthen your feet and ankles.

GOOD FOOT CARE

Your feet take a pounding, so treat them well. Wear shoes and socks that fit properly, since poorly fitting shoes and socks can contribute to many foot problems, from blisters to bunions. You should also keep your toenails trimmed properly to avoid painful ingrown toenails, and your feet well-lubricated while running to inhibit blistering. When you're not running, keep your feet as dry as possible to prevent itchy, burning fungal growth. If you do contract a fungus, there are over-the-counter and prescription anti-fungal medications available. For arch pain or weak ankles, try some of the exercises opposite. If arch pain persists, you may want to see a professional about getting orthotics (see p22).

Prevent ingrown toenails
Cut your toenails straight across to prevent ingrown toenails. Never cut into the sides of your nails, since this encourages the toenails to grow into the skin.

Prevent blisters
Massage petroleum jelly or heavy moisturizing cream into your feet to guard against blisters. This forms a barrier against chafing.

Foot and ankle strengthening exercises

The following exercises are wonderful for foot and ankle health, and can go a long way towards preventing injury. For maximum effectiveness, devote some time every day to performing these exercises.

Picking up marbles with your toes is a great all-over foot strengthener. Practise this exercise on each foot for about five minutes daily, since it challenges the muscles in your toes and arches. Be warned though: it's trickier than it looks!

Sit on a chair and roll your arch over a tennis ball. Do this for 3–5 minutes daily with each foot, since it breaks down tiny knots of scar tissue that inhibit full muscle contraction. Eliminating them loosens the foot muscles, allowing the arches to stretch out without straining.

Try this exercise to strengthen your arches and your ankles. Place a bunched-up hand towel on the ground, and hold onto a wall or heavy piece of furniture for balance. Grip the towel with your toes and lift it off the ground. While still holding the towel with your toes, circle your ankle clockwise for a full 360°. Reverse the direction, rotating your ankle anti-clockwise for a full 360°. Repeat 3–5 times. Switch legs and repeat.

Plantar fasciitis: causes and symptoms

Marked by extreme pain in the heel or the arch, plantar fasciitis is a very common and serious soft tissue affliction among runners. The pain is constant and increases when you walk, and tends to be worse after periods of inactivity.

A soft tissue called fascia forms the arch of your foot and connects your heel to the ball of your feet. Plantar fasciitis results when this fascia becomes overstretched or, in some extreme cases, tears. It is a stress point that is easily aggravated by the repetitive movement of running and, unfortunately, also happens to be an area of relatively little blood flow. This means it does not heal well from daily irritation and is predisposed to tearing.

Plantar fasciitis: prevention and correction

Plantar fasciitis is every runner's nightmare, since it requires total and immediate rest from running for up to six months. However, you should seek medical attention for this condition and follow the doctor's

advice. Throughout the healing period, you should regularly massage your foot (see *opposite*) and apply ice wrapped in cloth to the affected area. To prevent plantar fasciitis, cut back your running at the first hint of pain, and perform both exercises on page 107.

Don't feel as though you must give up all exercise for the six-month rest period. You can switch to alternative aerobic activities to get your exercise fix and keep fitness levels up. If you are lucky enough to have access to a pool, try swimming laps. My swimming technique is so bad that it is very easy for me to elevate my heart rate and get a good workout!

Heel spurs: causes and symptoms

This condition is accompanied by pain in the heel and/or the arch. The symptoms are almost exactly the same as those associated with plantar fasciitis. Heel spurs form when trauma causes the fascia to tear; the small drops of blood from the torn tissue then become part of the heel bone. The resulting heel spurs are actually new bone formations, which feel like small knots. They can cause great pain in the surrounding tissue when the foot makes contact with the ground.

Heel spurs: prevention and correction

To reduce swelling, apply ice wrapped in cloth to the affected area for ten minutes at a time. You can also use shock-absorbing heel pads or orthotics for arch support, which may prevent small fissures in the fascia. If they are extremely painful, you might need to have them removed surgically. To prevent heel spurs, wear shoes with good arch support, and after your runs, try the massage on page 107.

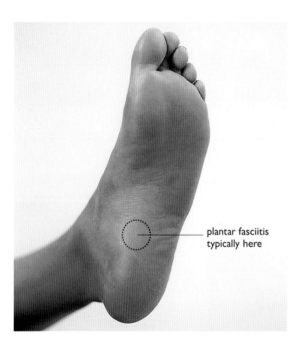

plantar fasciitis typically here

Plantar fasciitis: although similar to heel spurs, in plantar fasciitis the pain tends to be slightly closer to the arch (see *left*) than the heel. Heel spur pain centres around the heel itself.

Plantar fasciitis and heel spur exercises

The following exercises can help prevent and soothe both plantar fasciitis and heel spurs. The preventative stretch (*see below, left*) helps keep the tissue in the arches supple, thus protecting against microtears. The massage (*see below, right*) helps soothe plantar fasciitis, while preventing heel spurs from forming.

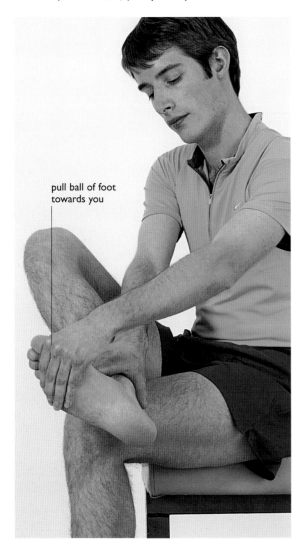

pull ball of foot towards you

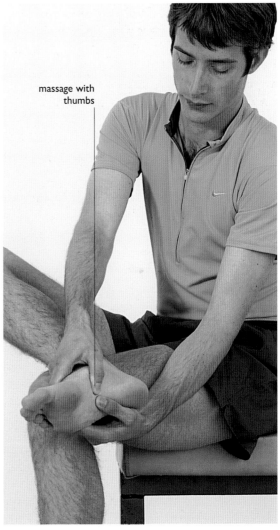

massage with thumbs

Preventative stretch

For supple arches, use this stretch daily to help prevent both plantar fasciitis and heel spurs. Cross one leg over the other, grasp the ball of your foot, and gently pull it towards you. Hold this position for 10–30 seconds, then rest. Switch feet and repeat twice on each foot.

Soothing massage

To help alleviate the pain of plantar fasciitis once it has happened, use the balls of your thumbs to massage the affected area when desired. To prevent the formation of heel spurs, massage the length and breadth of both arches for up to five minutes daily.

MAINTAIN PROGRAMME

If you have achieved an intermediate level of running but are not training for an upcoming race, self-coaching can help you to maintain your level of fitness without constantly pushing yourself further. This type of consistent training requires you to motivate yourself, as you do not have the end goal of a race to motivate you instead.

This progamme combines a mixture of time- and distance-based runs, interval training, and alternative forms of exercise such as cycling, swimming, and CrossFit™, which raise the heart rate and keep it elevated. There are four types of days, categorised by intensity – in other words, the percentage of your maximum heart rate, or MHR (see pp14–15) that you should aim for during training:

Rest days: Use these days to recover, and keep exercise to a minimum; at most, build your 1–2 weekly resistance training sessions into these days.

Easy/very easy days: Run/jog at up to 60 per cent MHR; you should remain well within conversational pace (see p27). These days help your body to recover, so try to consciously hold back.

Medium days: Train at around 60–70 per cent MHR. You may be slightly breathless at this level, but still capable of talking if necessary.

Hard/very hard days: Push yourself by training at up to 90 per cent MHR, depending on your level of fitness/ability. If you do not feel ready for interval training, try incorporating a weekly 16.1km (10 mile) run at the highest intensity you can comfortably manage.

A few points to remember. First, learn how to read your own body: being able to recognize the level of effort you are working at is key to an effective workout. Second, whenever the programme calls for "at least" a certain amount of training, continue only until you feel it is enough – do not overexert yourself. Finally, feel free to tailor this programme to your own needs. It is a guideline for maintaining your personal level of fitness. So long as you incorporate a good balance of easy and hard training days, interspersed with plenty of recovery time and some alternative forms of exercise (including twice-weekly resistance training sessions), you will be on track.

	Rest days		Medium days
	Easy/very easy days		Hard/very hard days

	Day 1	Day 2
WEEK 1	Easy run, 9.7km (6 miles)	Rest day + optional resistance training

	Day 8	Day 9
WEEK 2	At least 30 minutes alternative exercise (e.g. cross-training, cycling, swimming)	Run 9.7–11.3km (6–7 miles) at 60% MHR

	Day 15	Day 16
WEEK 3	Easy run, 11.3km (7 miles)	Run 9.7km (6 miles) at 60% MHR

	Day 22	Day 23
WEEK 4	Easy jog, 30 minutes + at least 30 minutes alternate exercise	Run 9.7km (6 miles) at 60% MHR

	Day 29	Day 30
WEEK 5	Easy jog, 30 minutes + at least 30 minutes alternate exercise	Run 12.9km (8 miles) at 60–70% of MHR

	Day 36	Day 37
WEEK 6	Easy jog, 30 minutes + at least 30 minutes alternate exercise	Run 14.5km (9 miles) at 70% MHR

	Day 43	Day 44
WEEK 7	Easy jog, 30 minutes + at least 30 minutes alternate exercise	Run 14.5km (9 miles) at 70% MHR

	Day 50	Day 51
WEEK 8	Easy jog, 30 minutes + at least 30 minutes alternate exercise	Run 14.5km (9 miles) at 70% MHR

Day 3	Day 4	Day 5	Day 6	Day 7
Run at least 9.7km (6 miles) at 60% MHR	Very easy jog, 40 minutes	Rest day + optional resistance training	Rest day + optional resistance training	3.2–4.8km (2–3 miles) warm-up jog; *2 x 2 minutes at 80% MHR (3-minute recovery)

Day 10	Day 11	Day 12	Day 13	Day 14
Easy jog, 40 minutes	At least 30 minutes alternative exercise (e.g. cross-training, cycling, swimming)	4.8km (3 miles) at an easy pace + 4.8km (3 miles) at 70–75% MHR	Rest day + optional resistance training	3.2km (2 miles) warm-up jog; *2 x 2 minutes at 90% MHR (2-minute recovery)

Day 17	Day 18	Day 19	Day 20	Day 21
At least 30 minutes alternative exercise (e.g. cross-training, cycling, swimming)	Rest day + optional resistance training	4.8km (3 miles) at an easy pace + 4.8km (3 miles) at 70–75% MHR	Very easy jog, 6.4km (4 miles)	3.2km (2 miles) warm-up jog; *2 x 2 minutes at 90% MHR (1.5-minute recovery)

Day 24	Day 25	Day 26	Day 27	Day 28
Easy jog, 40 minutes	Rest day + optional resistance training	4.8km (3 miles) at an easy pace + 4.8km (3 miles) at 70–75% MHR	Very easy jog, 6.4km (4 miles)	3.2km (2 miles) warm-up jog; *3 x 3 minutes at 80–90% MHR (3-minute recovery)

Day 31	Day 32	Day 33	Day 34	Day 35
Very easy jog, 40 minutes	Rest day + optional resistance training	Run 11.3km (7 miles) at 75% MHR	Very easy jog, 6.4km (4 miles)	3.2km (2 miles) warm-up jog; *4 x 3 minutes at 80–90% MHR (3-minute recovery)

Day 38	Day 39	Day 40	Day 41	Day 42
Very easy jog, 40 minutes	3.2km (2 miles) warm-up jog; *4 x 3 minutes at 80–90% MHR (3-minute recovery)	Rest day + optional resistance training	Very easy jog, 6.4km (4 miles)	3.2km (2 miles) warm-up jog; *6 x 1 minute at 90% MHR (1-minute recovery)

Day 45	Day 46	Day 47	Day 48	Day 49
Very easy jog, 40 minutes	3.2km (2 miles) warm-up jog; *2 x 2 minutes at 80–90% MHR (2-minute recovery)	Easy jog, 30 minutes + at least 30 minutes alternate exercise	Very easy jog, 6.4km (4 miles)	3.2km (2 miles) warm-up jog; *7 x 1 minute at 90% MHR (1-minute recovery)

Day 52	Day 53	Day 54	Day 55	Day 56
Very easy jog, 40 minutes	3.2km (2 miles) warm-up jog; *3 x 3, 2 x 2, and 2 x 1 minutes at 80–90% MHR (3-minute recovery)	Easy jog, 40 minutes	Run 8km (5 miles) at 60% MHR	3.2km (2 miles) warm-up jog; *8 x 1 minute at 90% MHR (1-minute recovery)

ADVANCED AND ELITE RUNNING

AFTER ABOUT A YEAR OF CONSISTENT RUNNING, YOU MAY FIND THAT YOUR PACE PLATEAUS, DESPITE INCREASING THE DISTANCES OF YOUR RUNS. I BELIEVE THIS IS LINKED TO THE LEVELLING OFF OF THE CAPACITY OF YOUR CARDIOVASCULAR SYSTEM – WHAT I CALL THE "ENERGY TRANSPORT SYSTEM." IN THIS REGARD, YOU ARE AS FIT AN AN INTERNATIONAL ATHLETE. NOW IT'S TIME TO INTRODUCE ANAEROBIC TRAINING TO YOUR WORKOUTS TO IMPROVE YOUR PERFORMANCE. THE GOOD NEWS IS THAT ONCE A WEEK IS ENOUGH TO SEE THE BENEFITS.

INTERVAL TRAINING

After about a year of consistent, easy aerobic training, many runners feel that their performances and cardiovascular efficiency level off, and that running greater distances no longer improves their speed. Interval training is the most efficient and productive tool I have experienced for increasing the overall pace of both your fast and slow running. This type of training works to improve the physiological process at the point of transfer, where the arteries and veins "meet" the muscles.

What is interval training?

Interval training involves running short bursts, each between 1 and 4 minutes long, at a pace sufficient to rase the heart rate to at least 80 per cent of the runner's predicted maximum heart rate, or even higher for very fit athletes (see p15 for more information on calculating your MHR). These bursts are known as intervals. Between each interval, the runner jogs (but does not walk) until his or her heart rate decreases to a conversational pace of about 120 BPM, or 60 per cent MHR. These periods are referred to as "recovery jogs".

How does it work?

Interval training works by improving your VO2 max, or the volume of oxygen your body can obtain and use while training at your MHR. High VO2 max values indicate high fitness levels, and this is what allows advanced and elite athletes to run faster and train more intensely than beginners. So as you improve your VO2 max through interval training, your ability to use oxygen will improve and your base aerobic pace increases, too.

Interval training will also help increase your aerobic training pace by improving what I call your "energy transport system". This refers to the efficiency with which your body transfers oxygen-rich blood to your muscles for use while training.

Focus on intensity for hard intervals: use association (see *box, opposite*) to concentrate on peak performance when running your hard intervals.

Structuring your training sessions

It makes common sense to structure your interval workouts in a way that generates a bit of anticipation and excitement, but does not lead to a feeling of dread. In other words, structure your workouts in such a way that they are demanding, but also realistic for your ability. Make interval training one of your "very hard" runs each week (see p67), to give yourself the reinforcement of doing just a little more than you had originally planned.

How do I do it?

You only need one interval training session per week; even elite athletes limit themselves to no more than twice a week. If you incorporate any more weekly sessions than this, you could be overtraining.

During your workout, your fast, hard segments can be as brief as one minute, or as long as four. Four minutes is the maximum amount of time you can run in an anaerobic state once you are in it. It takes a while during any interval to reach this state, so only in longer intervals will you be anaerobic for more than three minutes. For your recovery jog, slow down to your conversational pace until you reach 120 BPM. Your recovery can last up to twice as long as your hard intervals, but as mentioned opposite, these jogs will get successively shorter as you get stronger. The number of interval–recovery repetitions you run is variable and up to you: the stronger you become, the more repetitions you will be able to run.

ASSOCIATION AND DISSOCIATION

Psychologists have found that athletes generally enter one of two states while running: association and dissociation.

• When dissociating, an athlete lets his or her mind wander, and the run tends to fly by. An example of dissociation would be running with an MP3 player.

• Association is focusing on the task at hand. The athlete is "there" mentally, concentrating on peak performance, as in a sprint.

Dissociation is a perfect, relaxed state of mind for your easy runs, which should comprise 90 per cent of your workouts. Association is generally for that last 10 per cent of workouts – your hard runs. Interval training is a great way to practise association and dissociation. On hard repetitions, concentrate on what you wish to accomplish; really focus on running hard and fast. Then, as you ease into your recovery jog, let your mind wander and your body relax.

INTERVAL TRAINING FROM POLE TO POLE

You can interval train anywhere, whether it's in a gym, on a track, or on the road outside your house. Telegraph poles can be wonderful markers for your interval training, since they are usually positioned at regular intervals. Simply find a safe stretch of road lined with telegraph poles and start your training, alternating hard stretches of running with easy ones.

Easy jog
Jog very slowly to warm up your body first. Then ease into a conversational pace jog (RPE level six) for your slow interval. Jog the distance between three telegraph poles at this level of exertion.

Hard sprint
At the third pole, break into a hard run until you reach the next pole. You should be at RPE level eight (level nine for elite runners). Run the distance between two poles, then slow down for your recovery jog (*see left*). Repeat 5–6 times.

Interval training on a track: synthetic tracks provide an environment where all you have to do is focus on your fast bursts and recovery jogs: no hills, no dogs, no traffic.

Recovery is key

The recovery jog is the key here, not the speed of the intervals. With consistent interval training, your heart rate returns to 120 BPM more and more quickly in between repetitions, resulting in a faster overall pace. This faster pace is the result of increased efficiency at the muscle/blood vessel transfer point.

The pace at which you can run the intervals does not need to be much faster than the pace at which you may want to run a 5k race. Over time, your interval pace may slowly improve, but this is not as important as your recovery pace. During the first sessions, the total distance covered across all your intervals need only add up to 1.6km (1 mile). The furthest my intervals ever covered while I was training for the Olympic marathon only totalled 4.8km (3 miles).

Time or distance?

You can gauge the duration of your recovery intervals by time (see pp112–13) or by distance, depending on your preference. In determining the length of your hard, fast segments, you can also use time or distance, provided you can cover your chosen distance in fewer than three minutes. The important thing when meting out hard segments is that they are designated by constant markers of some kind. You may choose to train on a track (see below), or on a treadmill, which will display your distance and time on the computer console. Or, if you don't have access to either of these, you can find your own marking system, such as running from telegraph pole to telegraph pole along a quiet road (see p113).

Track work for interval training

Many elite runners prefer to interval train on synthetic tracks, since they are always flat, absorb much of the shock of impact, and have a standard perimeter of 400 metres (¼ mile). Most tracks have white markings that denote distances shorter than the perimeter as well.

A track is therefore the ideal place for interval training. I train on one in my home town, measuring my hard intervals in lap increments, and my recovery jogs in quarter-lap segments. However, you may choose to any combination of distances, depending on your preference and ability, using the white markers as your guides. Most towns have a track on a university or school campus, and often the institutions allow members of the public to use them. Be sure to always ask permission first, run with the flow of traffic, and stick to the outside lane.

Fartlek for fun: similar to interval training but less precise, fartlek (see opposite) involves changing your pace at random and non-rigid intervals during a run.

OPTIMUM INTERVAL TRAINING TIPS

Fast intervals should be no shorter than 200 metres (roughly 200 yards) and no longer than 1200 metres (¾ mile). The cumulative distance covered during fast intervals need not total more than 5km (3.1 miles) per session.

During hard segments, your level of exertion should be about level eight RPE (80 per cent MHR). Advanced and elite athletes may go as high as level nine RPE (90 per cent MHR).

Focus more on reducing the duration of your recovery jogs between hard repetitions than on increasing the speed of your hard segments.

One interval training session per week (or two at most) is all you need to increase fitness.

Hill training (see pp118–19) and fartlek (a less rigid form of interval training where you randomly vary fast- and slow-tempo running) are both nearly as effective as interval training for increasing pace.

INTERVAL TRAINING PROGRAMME

For intermediate and advanced runners who feel that their pace has levelled off and are looking to improve, interval training (*see pp114–17*) can be the solution. This type of training involves short bursts of intense sprinting followed by brief recovery jogs. It works by improving your body's ability to use oxygen while training at your anaerobic level, which in turn, helps to increase your base conversational pace.

Aim to decrease the duration of your recovery periods while slightly increasing the number and length of your hard segments. As you get stronger, you will be able to run more hard segments from which you will recover more quickly than before.

The programme on the right is meant to be used as a guideline, and not an exact formula for your workouts. Only one interval training workout per week (marked by an asterisk in the chart on the right) is required in order to improve your fitness. Advanced and elite athletes may incorporate two weekly sessions at the most. All other runs in this programme should be done at conversational pace.

Weeks 1–4 In the beginning, set yourself interval training goals that you know you can complete. Build up the length of your hard runs slowly, while simultaneously aiming to shorten your recovery time. For example, the first interval training session in the programme on the right suggests a 6.4km (4-mile) jog at conversational pace, followed by two hard two-minute interval sessions with one two-minute recovery jog in between. Feel free, however, to experiment with the suggested times and repetitions. It will probably take your body two weeks to adjust to interval training, but by the fourth week your recovery jogs will have become successively shorter and your hard segments should have increased in number and length.

Weeks 5–8 You should now be easing into your programme, and feeling more comfortable with interval training. Your base pace will most likely have improved, too. According to the two-week, two-month rule, after week eight, your body should be ready for the next challenge and primed to run a PB (personal best) race time.

| | Rest days |
| | Run days |

WEEK 1	**Day 1** Jog 9.7km (6 miles)	**Day 2** Rest day
WEEK 2	**Day 8** Rest day	**Day 9** Jog 9.7km (6 miles)
WEEK 3	**Day 15** Jog 10.5km (6.5 miles)	**Day 16** Rest day
WEEK 4	**Day 22** Rest day	**Day 23** Jog 8km (5 miles)
WEEK 5	**Day 29** Jog 9.7km (6 miles)	**Day 30** Rest day
WEEK 6	**Day 36** Rest day	**Day 37** Jog 8km (5 miles)
WEEK 7	**Day 43** Rest day	**Day 44** Jog 10.5km (6.5 miles)
WEEK 8	**Day 50** Jog 10.5km (6.5 miles)	**Day 51** Rest day

Day 3	Day 4	Day 5	Day 6	Day 7	Total
Jog 9.7km (6 miles)	Rest day	Jog 8km (5 miles)	Rest day	Jog 6.4km (4 miles); *2 x 2 minutes fast (2-minute recovery)	33.8km (21 miles)

Day 10	Day 11	Day 12	Day 13	Day 14	Total
Rest day	Jog 9.7km (6 miles)	Jog 8.6km (5.5 miles)	Rest day	Jog 6.4km (4 miles); *2 x 2 minutes fast (2-minute recovery)	34.6km (21.5 miles)

Day 17	Day 18	Day 19	Day 20	Day 21	Total
Jog 9.7km (6 miles)	Rest day	Jog 10.5km (6.5 miles)	Rest day	Jog 6.4km (4 miles); *2 x 2 minutes fast (1.5-minute recovery)	37km (23 miles)

Day 24	Day 25	Day 26	Day 27	Day 28	Total
Rest day	Jog 7.2km (4.5 miles)	Rest day	Jog 8km (5 miles)	Jog 6.4km (4 miles); *3 x 3 minutes fast (1.5-minute recovery)	29.8km (18.5 miles)

Day 31	Day 32	Day 33	Day 34	Day 35	Total
Jog 9.7km (6 miles)	Rest day	Jog 6.4km (4 miles)	Rest day	Jog 6.4km (4 miles); *4 x 3 minutes fast (1.5-minute recovery)	32.2km (20 miles)

Day 38	Day 39	Day 40	Day 41	Day 42	Total
Rest day	Jog 10.5km (6.5 miles)	Rest day	Jog 9.7km (6 miles)	Jog 6.4km (4 miles); *4 x 3 minutes fast (1.5-minute recovery)	34.6km (21.5 miles)

Day 45	Day 46	Day 47	Day 48	Day 49	Total
Rest day	Jog 10.5km (6.5 miles)	Jog 8km (5 miles)	Rest day	Jog 6.4km (4 miles); *4 x 3 minutes fast (1.5-minute recovery)	35.4km (22 miles)

Day 52	Day 53	Day 54	Day 55	Day 56	Total
Jog 9.7km (6 miles)	Rest day	Jog 10.5km (6.5 miles)	Rest day	Jog 6.4km (4 miles); *5 x 3 minutes fast (1.5-minute recovery)	37km (23 miles)

HILL TRAINING

Running up hills does more than make you feel rugged: it builds stamina and helps you to become a better sprinter, too. It is also a great training tactic for preventing injury, since your body is subjected to significantly less trauma from pounding than when running downhill or on a flat, zero-per cent gradient. For best results, search out slight gradients of no more than seven per cent. A steeper gradient will slow down your pace too much, and you'll hit a point of diminishing return.

Running uphill for power

Adding just one hill training session per week can do wonders for your stamina and sprinting ability. When running up hills, you are strengthening the same leg muscles that are responsible for fast sprinting. Running against the force of gravity builds strength, which will make you a powerful and fast runner on any gradient. It also improves your VO2 max, or the volume of oxygen your body can obtain and use while training at your MHR (see p112). A higher VO2 means that your body uses oxygen more efficiently, allowing you to maintain a relaxed and natural form while running at a faster pace than you would otherwise.

How to do it

Find a hill of about 100 to 400 metres (roughly 100 yards to ¼ mile) in distance and of no more than a seven-per cent gradient. It helps psychologically if you can see the top of the hill from the bottom. Run up the hill at an RPE of level eight. Your body will instinctively lean into the hill, and this is crucial for good sprinting. Lift your knees a bit higher and pump your arms harder than you would normally to gain momentum and power. Remember, you should be working hard here. Run as many repetitions up the hill as you can manage (2–5 climbs is standard), and recover in between by carefully jogging back down the hill. In the beginning, you may stop at the top of the hill to recover if you need to.

To advance your training, surge, or suddenly speed up, as you approach the top of the hill. Keep running hard beyond the crest of the hill and onto the flat before easing off your intensity to recover.

Exaggerate form for power: pump your arms and lift your knees a bit higher than you would normally to increase momentum as you run up hills.

Hill running: raise your game and improve
your VO2 max by incorporating hill training
to your running regimen.

SURFACES

Even though the high-tech design of today's running shoes offers a lot of protection from the pounding of running, the surface you run on is still very important. The shock of impact on hard, unyielding surfaces causes trauma to the body, and this added strain can delay recovery time at best, and at worst contribute to chronic pain and injury. The advice offered below can help you avoid injuries associated with running on hard surfaces.

Some surfaces are better than others

Running can be great for your general health, but if done incorrectly, it can be a very punishing to your musculoskeletal system. Every time your foot hits the ground, it does so with the impact of up to four times your body weight. Some surfaces send this shock ricocheting back up your leg, while other

surfaces absorb the shock, making for a relatively soft landing. Minimized impact through a soft and yielding contact with the ground allows for fast skeletal and muscular recovery. Therefore, common sense should tell you that you should run on surfaces that absorb as much of the shock of impact as possible. No surface is perfect, but some are better than others for shock absorption (*for a list of surfaces, see opposite*).

Variation is key

To minimize your risk of injury, you must vary your routes and surfaces regularly. If you constantly run on the same surface day after day, your legs will be repeatedly hitting the ground in exactly the same way every time you run; this makes your body vulnerable to injury. This pattern wears down bone, muscle, and cartilage, creating an injury groove, or an orthopaedic groove that may lead to injury. So, in addition to training on soft surfaces as much as possible, make it a point to vary your surface from time to time. These changes do not have to be extreme. If you normally run on a dirt trail through a park, you could occasionally jog on the grass next to your regular path. Any variation is beneficial, as long as you can sense that it is getting you out of that injury groove.

Choose your surface wisely: running on a soft surface that absorbs shock, such as a dirt trail, can help minimize your chance of injury.

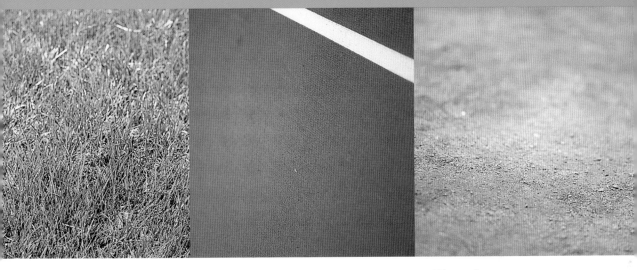

Grass
If it is even, flat, and manicured, grass can be an ideal running surface. It is soft and easy on the body, but not so soft that it places undue strain on your muscles. Be sure to avoid lumpy grass, though.

Track
Synthetic running track can be a wonderful surface to run on because it is designed to absorb shock. The track material is structured to suction and rebound at the same time.

Dirt path
Trails or dirt paths can be an excellent choice of running surface, since they are both relatively soft. Watch your footing, though, as you could trip over rocks and exposed tree roots.

Sand
Flat, firm sand can be a great surface to run on. It absorbs shock, and you can even run barefoot. Avoid soft or uneven sand, though, since it can lead to strained calf muscles and injury.

Tarmac
Slightly more absorbent than concrete, particularly in the summer months, this surface is always preferable to concrete. It is still hard on the body, though, so try to avoid it as much as you can.

Concrete
This is the hardest surface you can run on, absorbing almost none of the shock of impact. Concrete should be avoided whenever possible.

ROUTES AND ROUTINES

Most runners are creatures of habit, and therefore find themselves settling into one or two "standard routes" that they take every time they run. However, like running on the same surface every day, running the same course all the time can take its toll in the form of repetitive strain injury. Prevent your regular route from becoming the route to injury by integrating new courses into your running repertoire.

Three routes are better than two

To avoid injury associated with running the same route day after day, you should aim to have three stock courses and run them interchangeably. Get to know these courses well so you feel comfortable with them. This will allow you to dissociate, letting your mind wander so the time passes quickly. You will also feel relaxed while running a known, habitual route, without the drawback of running in the same injury groove each day.

Your multi-route catalogue will also work different muscles in different ways, thereby giving you a more challenging workout than if you had

The benefits of variety: try to break out of the habit of running one or two routine courses. Having three runs, of varying locale and difficulty, is better for your body than two.

simply run your two standard loops. Your routes should also be of varying levels of difficulty, and, if possible, through different environments to counteract boredom.

It is important that you choose three routes that you will enjoy running, so running them becomes something you look forward to. You can then pick and choose which run you wish to do – easy, intermediate, or hard – depending on how you feel.

Your first run could be a short and easy one through a park, on a soft, shock-absorbing surface, such as grass or dirt. For your second route, plan a middle-distance run on the pavement through your neighbourhood. This run should be slightly harder than your first run. Your third route might be a long one, on a trail through the woods. It should be the most difficult of the three, and it may even include some hills.

Small variations for creatures of habit

You need not radically overhaul your running routes to avoid the injuries associated with running in the same groove every day. If you cannot face adding a new route to your one or two standard loops, change your existing ones in small ways instead. For example, run your usual training loop in the opposite direction.

If you see another type of surface nearby while on your course, try running on it for a little while to break up the usual stress patterns. You could even try running on the other side of the road, or simply vary the length of your typical loop. Cut it short some days and walk for the last ten minutes, and stretch it out on other days, depending on how you feel. Any variation is good for your body, as long as you can sense that it is getting you out of that injury groove.

Using a treadmill

Shake up your usual running routine by using a treadmill. The treadmill belt absorbs more shock than most surfaces, and since the belt moves with you, it is slightly easier on your body than road running.

1 Stand with your feet on the sides of the machine, placing your feet on either side of the central belt. Press the start button.

2 Hold on to the side bars and begin to walk on the belt as it starts to move. Press the relevant button to increase your speed gradually.

3 Release the side bars and begin to jog or run, depending on your desired speed. To slow down or stop, press the relevant buttons on the console.

BREATHING

If you are breathing efficiently, you will not even be aware of it. The trick is to stay relaxed, but this is sometimes harder than it sounds. Some people actually become tense and stressed while running, which causes them to hyperventilate. If, while running at your normal conversational pace, you have difficulty getting enough oxygen, try the following exercises to dissipate tension and normalize breathing.

Is there a wrong way to breathe?

There is no wrong way to breathe while running, and the most effective way you can get oxygen into your lungs, be it through your mouth, nose, or both, is the best method for you. Remember, everyone is an expert when it comes to breathing, as long as you stay relaxed.

Relaxed breathing on easy runs

During easy, conversational pace runs, you should not even notice how you are breathing, but the key is to stay relaxed. To avoid tension, which can lead to irregular breathing patterns, perform the relaxation exercise opposite just before you begin your run.

Relaxed breathing on hard runs

On hard runs, breathing is necessarily a bit more laboured. However, do not fixate on this, since it can be distracting and cause you to lose your mental focus. Instead, try resetting your breathing rhythm with what I call the "cleansing breath" (*see below*). If you work on relaxing while running hard, your natural breathing patterns will fall into place.

THE CLEANSING BREATH

Sometimes when you are training hard, your body tenses up, which inhibits your natural form and comfortable running. When this happens, I find that it is helpful to take a deep breath while running, and then exhale fully to relax and reset my natural breathing. This cleansing breath will help you to resume comfortable breathing, too. As you exhale, let your arms dangle relaxed by your sides for a few strides; then allow them to come up to where they "want" to go as you ease back into your natural running form.

inhale deeply

exhale fully

Breathing for relaxation

Many runners find that they need to work on staying relaxed, and one of the best ways to do this is by taking a few deep breaths before embarking on your warm-up jog. This exercise only takes a minute, but the effects on your mind and body are immeasurable.

2 Let your arms and shoulders drop as you exhale for three counts, expelling the carbon dioxide from your lungs. Repeat this sequence 3–5 times, or until you feel loose and relaxed.

1 Stand with your feet hip-width apart, with your arms relaxed by your sides. Breathe in deeply for three counts, expanding your chest fully as you lift your shoulders up and back.

SAFETY AND VISIBILITY

I am invisible when I run, so "accommodating and alive" is my motto, and it should be yours, too. Whenever you come to an intersection and cross a street, assume that the driver cannot see you, even if you make eye contact. A driver's mistake could cost you your limbs or your life. In deserted areas, always run in pairs or groups, since a lone runner could become a victim of unwanted attention or aggression.

Stay alert and dress appropriately

The old saying that you can be "dead right" in a right-of-way situation truly applies to the interaction of runners and vehicles. When running at night, or in the dark hours of the early morning, avoid crossing roads, keep to the pavement, and try to seek out lighted areas. I also highly recommend wearing blinking battery-powered lights or reflective clothing. These safety measures should not slacken your vigilance, since they are just attention-getters for drivers. The fact that a driver senses something is in his or her path does not mean they know you are there: they could still hit you.

Protect yourself

Never run alone at night. Find at least one partner to join you on your run, and never run through a remote area. Joggers at night in deserted locations can be very conspicuous, and sadly, there are people out there who target lone runners for any number of unpleasant reasons. Minimize your risks by avoiding these areas and running in groups.

People who choose to run at night should also carry an alarm mechanism of some sort – the louder and more obnoxious, the better. These devices are inexpensive and widely available. Pedometers often come with a personal alarm.

Always carry your phone with you, in case you need to make an emergency call. Some running apps are also available that track your movements in real time and share them with a chosen contact, so they know where to find you in case anything happens.

< Run with a friend: it's always safest to run with a partner or a group, especially if you are a woman. Running on your own leaves you vulnerable to the wrong kind of attention.

Reflective gear is a must: when running at night, or in the early hours of the morning, always wear reflective garments and stay alert. >

SAFETY TIPS FOR NIGHT RUNNING

Always wear reflective clothing.

Run on the side of the road facing oncoming traffic, so you can see cars coming towards you.

Choose a route that does not cross streets.

Never run alone, especially if you are a woman.

Carry a mobile phone with emergency numbers saved to your contacts list.

Carry a personal alarm with you.

Always give vehicles a wide berth and the right of way.

Never run through a remote area where you may be too far from help.

Choose a familiar course to avoid getting lost.

RACING

RACING CAN BE FUN NO MATTER WHAT YOUR LEVEL OF ABILITY. IT PROVIDES AN IMMEDIATE SOURCE OF SATISFACTION AND GIVES YOU A SERIES OF BENCHMARKS ON WHICH TO BASE YOUR TRAINING. I CONSIDER ANY RACE OF MORE THAN 1.6KM (1 MILE) TO BE A DISTANCE EVENT. JUST AS ONE OF THE GOALS OF INTERVAL TRAINING IS TO GET YOUR LEGS USED TO MOVING AT A FASTER PACE THAN YOU WOULD RUN NORMALLY, THERE IS AN ADAPTIVE TRAINING EFFECT FROM RACING AT DISTANCES SHORTER THAN YOUR RACE OF CHOICE. I ALWAYS THINK OF SHORT RACES AS TRAINING FOR MY LONGER EVENTS.

RACE PREPARATION

You've done all of your physical training, and now it's time to psychologically prepare for the event. During these final two weeks before your event, you cannot improve your fitness, regardless of how much you train. Now the key is to maintain as much of your normal routine as possible, but on a scaled-back level. Review your logs to remind yourself that you have indeed put in all the hard work necessary to perform well on race day.

Review your logs and set your goal

Take time to review your training log. It will psychologically reinforce the notion that you have done all the required training and are ready for your event. It will also reflect all your hard-earned improvements. Use your logs to determine what you think you are capable of on race day.

A safe race pace goal would be the same pace you averaged on your long training runs. At the back of your mind, you could have a "reach" goal of about one minute per 1.6km (1 mile) faster than the pace of your long training runs (see p94). Calculate your times, or splits, at different points throughout the race at both your safe and reach paces. You can then transfer this information to a splits bracelet (see below), which you can wear while racing.

A bit of uncertainty about how you will do on race day is normal and beneficial. To boost your morale, review your racing logs for a day that you felt a bit nervous about your performance, and then exceeded your expectations.

Don't try anything new

In the two-week run-up to your race, do not try anything new. Maintain as much of your normal routine as possible, but scaled down

---

SPLIT TIMES

Split times tell runners what their times should be at critical points along the course, in order to maintain their ideal pace. Many runners' websites offer pre-calculated splits for different distances and paces. You can also calculate your own splits: first, determine your goal race pace per kilometre or mile in minutes, then multiply that number by each kilometre or mile you want to monitor.

For the race itself, you can print off splits as a "splits bracelet" (see right): a paper wristband to be worn during the race so you can make sure that you are hitting your targets. Some fitness trackers and apps can also alert you in real time as you pass each split point, using GPS. However, these can be inaccurate if the GPS function is obstructed, so rely on them with caution.

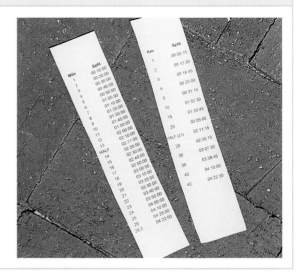

(see *Tapering, pp134–35*). This includes no major changes in diet, training, sleep habits, avoidable stress levels, and especially clothing and footwear. Any changes to your normal routine could compromise your performance. The temptation to buy a new pair of shoes before your race is normal: it is only natural to be on the lookout for something that might help you achieve your goal. Shop if you want, buy if you must, but do not use any of your purchases until after the race!

Get familiar and visualize

For races up to 14.5km (9 miles), walk or cycle your course two days before the event. If you live near your marathon course, jog the last 10km (6.2 miles) at an easy pace a week before. Most

Preview the course: for races up to 14.5km (9 miles), walk or slowly jog the course two days before the race. The familiarity of the course will help dissipate nervousness on the big day.

runners find this last part of the race to be the toughest. Never drive or walk the whole marathon course, though: it takes a long time to cover 42.1km (26.2 miles), and the memory of it will do you more mental harm than good.

If you do not live near your course, find a map and make a note of its hills. As you familiarize yourself with your course, visualize yourself successfully completing the race. When you get out there on race day, you'll find that it seems a little bit more familiar than it would otherwise.

TAPERING YOUR TRAINING

Training hard in the two weeks prior to your race, particularly if it is a marathon, will not increase your fitness. In fact, you could spend this time in bed doing nothing at all, and it would still not decrease your fitness. My motto for these two weeks is that less training is indeed better. Taper, or scale back, your running during this period to avoid pre-race injury, maximize glycogen storage, and preserve muscular freshness.

Why taper your training?

Tapering involves scaling back your running distance and effort level, and many world records have been set when, because of minor injuries, runners have had to taper their training in the two weeks prior to a race.

These athletes were forced to ease off their training, and then they went on to surpass everyone's expectations. The fact is, training hard two weeks before a race can only hurt you physically. It can cause injury, tear down muscles and deplete them of glycogen. Tapering your training protects your body from last-minute injury. It also gives your body a well-deserved rest, during which you will lose none of your fitness.

How do I do it?

As I said before, you could theoretically refrain from running completely during these final two weeks and still retain your physical fitness, but the mental side of this is another story. Many runners, including me, continue to train for psychological reasons. This satisfies a mental urge to exercise and prepare, despite the fact that there are no physical advantages.

TAPERING CHART

You cannot improve your fitness in the two-week run-up to your race, and if you're not careful, you could actually impede your performance on race day. To avoid this, you must taper or scale back your running as much as possible.

See the chart on the right for an example of how to taper your regimen. The top row represents a runner's final week of hard training before a marathon. The two rows below show what two weeks of tapered training should look like. Remember, though, that this is only an outline of the most training you could safely do in the two weeks prior to your race; this is more for your peace of mind than your fitness! Except where otherwise noted, all of these runs are meant to be easy workouts done at conversational pace.

Week	Sunday	Monday
Hard training	8km (5 miles)	Rest day
Tapering week 1	9.7km (6 miles)	Rest day
Tapering week 2	9.7km (6 miles)	9.7km (6 miles)

Finding your own balance between total rest and the amount of exercise you need in order to *feel* prepared is key.

Every runner is different, with varying psychological requirements for exercise. How much you taper your training is therefore a subjective thing, so scale it down to whatever feels reasonable for you. A good general guideline for tapering, which I use myself, is to scale back your distance and intensity by 30 per cent.

So, if you had been averaging 64.4km (40 miles) per week in training, you should reduce this distance to no more than 45km (28 miles) per week of easy running at conversational pace. You may want to go for a run while listening to music to ensure that you are dissociating (see p113), and thereby running easily. This will not deplete glycogen stores or hinder your performance on race day.

Less running is better before a race: scale back your training in distance and exertion. All runs you do in this two-week period should be easy and at conversational pace.

Tuesday	Wednesday	Thursday	Friday	Saturday	Total
11.3km (7 miles)	Rest day	12.9km (8 miles)	Rest day	32.2km (20 miles) (hard workout)	64.4km (40 miles)
9.7km (6 miles)	9.7km (6 miles)	Rest day	9.7km (6 miles)	6.4km (4 miles)	45km (28 miles)
9.7km (6 miles)	9.7km (6 miles)	Rest day	6.4km (4 miles)	Rest day	45km (28 miles)

EATING TO WIN

What you eat during the two weeks prior to a race can play just as big a role in your preparation as your training. However, this does not mean that you should embark on a special diet: now is not the time to make sweeping changes. My first rule of eating for racing is not to eat anything new. Aim instead to taper your general calorie intake by 30 per cent, while increasing consumption of complex carbohydrates in your existing diet.

Moderation and nothing new

As with your training, running gear, and sleeping habits, you should not change your diet just before you race. If you have trained properly and maintained a healthy, balanced diet comprised of complex carbohydrates, protein, fruits, and vegetables (see pp72–5), stick with what you know. Your body may react badly to changes, which could spell disaster during the race for a number of reasons, ranging from constipation to weight gain to feeling generally sick.

No fancy diet required: stick with the foods you know during this final period before the race. While you are tapering your training, fewer calories and more complex carbohydrates are needed.

If you are racing abroad, remember that simple food is safest. You may have trouble finding your normal fare, so it is a good idea to bring some wholemeal bread, fruit, and vegetables with you, just in case these items are not readily available. In a pinch, you can then enjoy a simple meal in your hotel room.

Scale back your intake

In the two weeks prior to your race, you will be tapering your training, so common sense says you should consume fewer calories than before. Aim to strike a balance that feels right for you, though. Use caution when considering your racing diet,

especially during the last three days before a marathon. If you eat too little during this period, you may experience a profound energy drop around 32.2km (20 miles) and "hit the wall" (see box, right), as runners call it.

That said, eating too much during the two-week tapering period may cause constipation or weight gain that you will have to carry during the race. A rule of thumb is to scale back your food intake by about 30 per cent during the two weeks before the race. Then, during the last three days before the race, carbo-load, which involves consuming a larger percentage of your calories from carbohydrates than before (see box, right). This will top off glycogen stores without giving your body time to turn the extra calories into stored fat. On the morning of the race, eat your typical breakfast roughly two hours before the start of the race, and some energy gel 30 minutes before the start, if you've used this during training. This will leave you feeling energized and ready to run.

THE WALL AND CARBO-LOADING

"Hitting the wall" happens to most marathon runners at some point during their running career. It is marked by a sudden and dramatic drop in energy, where every step is a challenge. Most marathon runners hit the metaphorical wall around 32.2km (20 miles) in, when the body has been depleted of its stored glycogen limit. It must then use its less efficient sources of fuel: fat and protein. This slows your pace and makes running seem harder than it was before. The change is so dramatic you may think you are going even more slowly than you actually are. If you reach this stage during a race, energy gels or sports drinks can help give you a boost to the finish line (see p137).

Carbo-loading can help prevent you from from hitting the wall in the first place. It involves tapering your running (see pp132–33), while increasing your carbohydrate intake to up to 70 per cent of your daily calories during the three days prior to the event. This ensures that you have as much glycogen as possible available to use as your primary energy source. Enhance this process by taking a fairly hard training run of no more than 5km (3.1 miles) just before you begin carbo-loading: this slight depletion will prime you for storing new glycogen. After three days of carbo-loading, your energy fuel tanks should be full.

THE FINAL RUN-UP

Feeling disorganized or unprepared before a race can be extremely distracting. Even if you have kept a gruelling training schedule, it's often the little things, such as too few safety pins or forgetting your watch, that can undermine your race performance. The three days prior to your race require foresight and preparation, but luckily this section will eliminate some of the guesswork. Consult the following pages for practical racing preparation tips and advice.

Food and hydration

The three days prior to your race are critical for a strong run. This is the time to make certain that you are well-nourished. For races shorter than a marathon, simply maintain your usual diet, and refrain from introducing any new eating habits.

If you are running a marathon, during the previous two weeks you should have been tapering your training and scaling back your calorie intake by about 30 per cent. During this final three-day period, you should increase your food intake and begin to carbo-load (*see box, p135*), obtaining 70 per cent of your calories from carbohydrates, to top off glycogen stores.

Aim to consume the equivalent of six to eight glasses of water daily during these final three days. On the day of the race, drink a tall glass of water about 60–90 minutes before the start. Any later than this and you may have to use the toilet – any earlier and your body will have already used the water.

ITEMS TO GATHER THE DAY BEFORE A RACE

Your number, safety pins, and your watch are essentials for the race, but I also recommend bringing a splits bracelet, a bin liner for warmth, and petroleum jelly. You might also bring a portable water bottle and energy gel. If you are renting a ChampionChip® to clock your exact time, you will need to pick it up from race headquarters the day before your race.

A water bottle and energy gel are not required, but if you wish to bring them, now is the time to have them on hand.

A digital watch will help you keep track of your time.

Use safety pins to fasten your race number to your shirt. You should have your received your number in the post prior to the race.

A splits bracelet for keeping track of your pace may have been included in your race pack. If not, you can print one out from a running website.

Wear a bin liner over your running gear before the race – you can discard it at the starting line. It will keep you warm and preserve your energy for the race.

Use petroleum jelly to lubricate any areas that may chafe, including underarms, breasts or nipples, feet, and inner thighs.

Sleep for success

The night before a race, it's common for runners to suffer from minor insomnia. Luckily, it's not the night before the race that's crucial for a good night's sleep, but the night before that. Don't despair, however, if you have trouble sleeping two nights before the race. It's usually enough to lie very still in bed and at least rest your body. This is not a licence to go out for a night on the town before the race, since excess stimulation in any form will only impair your performance on race day. The run-up to the race will provide you with all the adrenaline you can handle. Rest and relaxation is really what you need to do your best.

What you'll need

The night before the race you'll need to gather together a few items (see box, below left) including your race numbers and at least eight safety pins to secure them to the front and back of your shirt.

You'll also need petroleum jelly for lubricating areas susceptible to chafing, and your splits bracelet to keep track of your predicted pace. I also recommend wearing a digital watch when racing. The clock starts when the first runner crosses the starting line, and you may not cross it for a few minutes. Your own watch can be a great motivator. Use it to monitor your progress, and cross-check your time with your splits bracelet whenever you wish. A ChampionChip® (see p24) will also give your precise splits, but not until the race has ended.

Harness that nervous energy!

Nervousness and poor weather may leave you shivering before the race. Channel this energy instead into a strong performance in the first half of the race. Wear a plastic bin liner over your shorts and T-shirt just before the race. It will keep you warm and prevent shivering at the starting line, and you can discard it just before the race begins.

SPORTS FOODS AND DRINKS

You do not need to invest in sports foods to race well; a piece of fruit or a bottle of water mixed with a little rock salt can work just as well. However, many races offer sports drinks on the course, and you should take them when offered, if you've used them during training. If you still want to eat sports foods, here are some tips on when and how to eat them.

Sports drinks
Well-organized races will have drink stations throughout, offering both sports drinks and water to keep you hydrated and give you a boost.

Energy gel
Carrying gel with you while racing is not necessary. Eat some before the race instead and always with water, in order to digest the carbohydrates.

Energy bars
Eat an energy bar about an hour before the race, but not during it. A dry mouth may leave you unable to chew one during the race.

BEFORE THE RACE

Before the race, you will undoubtedly feel a bit of nervousness, and this is completely normal. If you know what to expect, however, you can anticipate this stress and avoid it. Make sure you know exactly where to go on race day, and leave yourself plenty of time to get to the starting line and warm up properly. Rushing before you even get to the race can put you at a big psychological disadvantage. Use the tips below to head off any other chances for pre-race nerves.

Pro-active measures

There are a few things I recommend you do before a race. For a half-marathon or longer, lubricate areas prone to chafing, such as feet, underarms, inner thighs, and nipples with petroleum jelly. Also apply sunscreen to exposed skin.

You should also establish a landmark near the finish line to meet your friends and family. It can get very crowded near the finish, and you won't feel like walking very far after the race – and you might not be thinking clearly, either.

Positive ritual in warming up

To minimize nervousness and pre-race jitters, you should warm up for your race in the same way that you warm up for a regular run. Your typical warm-up is a subtle form of positive ritual that helps you control your sympathetic nervous system. Straying from your normal routine tells your body that something unusual is happening, which activates your sympathetic nervous system. This elevates your heart rate and blood pressure, causing stress hormones to be released into the bloodstream.

To prevent this, simply warm up in the way you always have. Beginners running relatively short races need only to jog very slowly for 1–3 minutes, 15 minutes before the race starts. For races longer than 5km (3.1 miles), jog for 10–15 minutes at a very slow pace, 30 minutes prior to the start. Finish no less than ten minutes before the race

begins. If you have a particular warm-up method, such as running fast for one minute and then slow for three, then do that. This is part of your positive ritual.

Finding your place in the crowd

Many races have a staggered start. Racers are broken into groups by their estimated finish time (e.g. four hours), with the fastest runners starting first and slowest runners starting last. A designated pace-maker will run the exact estimated time with each group. Calculate your splits and finish time in advance (see p130) to determine which time group you should be running with.

> ### RACE-DAY TRICKS
>
> **Wear broken-in shoes.** New ones are an unknown quantity and may cause blistering and intense pain.
>
> **Join the queue** for the toilet 30–45 minutes in advance. The queues can get very long 20 minutes before the race.
>
> **Dissociate** and go relatively easy for the first half of the race to avoid burning out. Associate in the second half, when the going gets tough.
>
> **The opposition** is thinking about you, rather than themselves, on race day. The trick is for you to think about yourself, without thinking about them.

TIME TO WARM UP

Being organized can save you hassle and stress
before the race. Get to the starting line early
so you can warm up properly before you race.

Get ready early by putting on your number as soon as possible.

1795

Wear your usual running shoes to prevent blisters.

DURING THE RACE

You've put in the required training and now you're ready for the event. In addition to the psychological tools you've used during training, such as visualization (*see pp68–69*) and association and dissociation (*see p113*), there are a few other tips and tactics you can use during the race to achieve your fastest race time, or personal best (PB). The racing hints on pages 142–145 will give you a mental and physical advantage over your competitors.

Take it slow at the beginning

When the race starts, you'll feel a huge surge of adrenaline, and you may get caught up in the moment. This can translate as running too fast for the first quarter, or even half, of the race. Avoid starting out too fast at all costs. You may feel great at first, but if you are running much faster than you thought you could, it's likely that you'll burn out and be unable to maintain your speed. In the worst-case scenario, you may not even have the energy to finish. Try to stay as close to your splits as possible.

Always take drinks where offered

During races of half-marathon and longer distances, you will see drink stations en route. Do not think stopping for an energy drink and a cup of water will slow you down. These pit-stops will keep you hydrated and will give you much-needed glucose for energy, both of which will help you in the long term. Always take advantage of them whenever you are feeling thirsty to avoid dehydration, but be careful not to over-hydrate (see *pp76–77*).

Race tactics

There are three big tricks you can use to shave seconds, and even minutes, off your finish time. Drafting (see *opposite*) is running behind someone, ¾ off their shoulder, and it can save up to seven per cent of your race energy output by minimizing your air friction. Running the tangents (see *p143*)

> ### TIPS TO REMEMBER
>
> **Don't start too fast.** This will only come back to haunt (and exhaust) you. Stay focused on your predicted splits.
>
> **Accept drinks** and energy foods wherever offered. The time you lose to drink or eat will be made up for by the surge of hydration and energy provided.
>
> **Draft** behind a competitor or your pace-maker. Run ¾ off his or her shoulder. Running in his or her wake can reduce friction of the air against your body, which conserves energy. Towards the end of the race, you'll be ready to surge (see *below*).
>
> **Run the tangents** to shorten the distance of your race, and subsequently improve your race time. The professionals do it, so why shouldn't you?
>
> **Occasionally surge** by slightly increasing the pace of the group you're running with. Your interval training will help you to recover more quickly than your competitors.

---

is running the shortest distance between two points (e.g. through curves in the course), which can shorten the distance you cover. It can thereby give you a faster finish time than your non-tangent-running competitors. The third tactic is surging (see *p142*), which is a skill honed through interval training. It involves periodically increasing your "pack's" pace beyond anaerobic threshold, so as to tire out your competitors. Many Olympic marathons are won by racers who are successful at surging.

Drafting

Let your competitor create a passageway of calm air through which you can run. Since the runner in front will be hitting the stream of air first, he or she will minimize air friction for you. You'll therefore save energy while also running faster. Find a racer who is only slightly faster than you, and fall in just behind his or her shoulder. Maintain a courtesy distance of about 1.5 metres (5 feet).

Surging

Dedicated interval training lends itself to successful surging. They both involve briefly increasing base pace to an anaerobic level, followed by a period of recovery. If you're a strong surger who is capable of quick recovery, surging can help you to beat your competitors and gain a psychological advantage.

1 During a race, you will have settled into a base race pace with a group of runners of similar ability. Run easily with the pack and, when you feel ready, increase your own pace slightly. You should be easing into your anaerobic zone, and the pack will most likely move with you. Slow down after three minutes, returning to your base pace.

2 After a brief recovery jog at conversational pace, surge again (see step 1). Interval work from your training should have improved your ability to recover, which may give you an advantage over your competitors. Runners in your pack who have a slow recovery time will be unable to keep up with their stronger counterparts.

Running the tangents

Simple mathematics tells us that a straight line is the shortest distance between two points. This same concept holds true for racing, so use this knowledge to your advantage. When approaching a bend in the course, cut straight through it (*see runner, front*), rather than hugging the curve (*see runner, behind*).

AFTER THE RACE

After pushing yourself to the limit during your race, it is important that you cool down properly. As in training, walking or jogging slowly, followed by some light stretching, is the best and most efficient way to flush out lactic acid and other toxins and to restore your body's equilibrium. After a race such as a marathon, you may feel so exhausted that you won't want to cool down, and this is precisely the reason that you should.

Races up to a half-marathon

After racing distances of 21km (13.1 miles) or less, you should walk or jog very slowly for at least ten minutes to allow your heart rate to return to normal. Follow your cool-down walk or jog with a series of light stretches (see pp42–49) to prevent muscular stiffness the next day. Then wrap up warm, drink some water, and relax.

Stay warm after a marathon

When you cross the finish line of a marathon, a race official will hand you a plastic blanket. Even if you don't want it now, you will later. Your body temperature will drop quickly after the race, and that blanket may help prevent hypothermia.

Keep moving

Cooling down after your race is essential: if you neglect your body's needs now, you will undoubtedly regret it later. I've seen many runners unwisely sit down immediately after finishing a marathon, only to be unable to stand up again due to seized-up muscles. To prevent this, take a very slow 10–15 minute jog, preferably with some other runners from the race. This sociable cool-down will allow your body to flush out the lactic acid in your legs, while also giving you chance to tell your race story. Follow your cool-down jog with a full series of stretches (see pp42–49) to speed the healing process.

Eat and drink

Food may be the last thing on your mind after a gruelling race, but try to make yourself eat something within two hours of finishing the race. Complex carbohydrates, such as wholemeal bread or pretzels, will boost low blood-sugar levels, and protein, such as a smoothie or some turkey, will help your muscles repair themselves. If you cannot handle the idea of food, try eating an energy bar, or at the very least have a sports drink to restore your lost minerals such as salt. Water is also essential after the race. Your body will take a few days to fully rehydrate itself, so be patient and consistently consume the equivalent of six to eight glasses of water daily.

Massage and rest

Most marathons (and some half-marathons) offer post-race sports massage services for a reasonable price. Many runners believe that these massages can help flush out lactic acid from your muscles. If you can brave the long queues to get one, it's a nice reward for completing your race.

Above all, though, your body needs rest to repair itself. Races are demanding events, so after you've cooled down and had something to eat and drink, sit back, relax, and enjoy your achievement.

Wrap up to prevent a chill: after a marathon, your body will cool down rapidly. Take the plastic blanket offered to you by race officials to stay warm.

THE FIRST WEEK AFTER THE RACE

A marathon can be very hard on your body, so it's natural to feel a little unwell afterwards. Do not run at all during the week following the race. Your body is in recovery mode, and running too soon can contribute to injury. Here are a few things to expect in the seven days following the race:

• extreme muscular soreness; difficulty walking.

• depressed immune system; you may even catch a cold!

• dehydration, accompanied by swollen legs and feet.

• post-race depression is also common among marathon runners.

RE-BUILDING YOUR TRAINING

After your race, particularly if it's a marathon, your body has most likely been pushed to its limit. It is therefore critical that you give your body enough time to recover from this trauma. This means taking an adequate number of rest days and building up your running slowly. If you don't listen to your body by giving it enough rest, you could risk long-term injury. Read on for advice on how to resume your running safely and effectively.

Reverse your tapering to re-build

We're all different, so the time it takes you to recover from a race may be different from that of your running partner. Regardless, this is not the time to take chances with your body, so it's best to play it safe.

The saying goes that you should take a recovery day for each 1.6km (1 mile) of your race. Following a marathon, this translates as roughly 3–5 weeks of recovery time. Do not skimp on your recovery –

you may do your body more harm than good. The first week after your race, you should refrain completely from running and all but the very gentlest of training (e.g. walking). For the following 2–4 weeks, reverse your tapering programme (see pp132–33), running easily at conversational pace and crosstraining instead where necessary.

Take it slow: do not run at all during the first week after the race; gentle exercise, such as walking, light resistance training, or cycling is preferable during this seven-day period.

POST-MARATHON SAMPLE BUILD-UP CHART

Weeks	1	2	3	4	5
Day 1	Race day	Rest day	Jog 8km (5 miles)	Jog 8km (5 miles)	Jog 9.7km (6 miles)
Day 2	Rest day	Cycle 30 minutes	Jog 4.8km (3 miles)	Jog 8km (5 miles)	Jog 9.7km (6 miles)
Day 3	Rest day	Rest day	Rest day	Rest day	Swim 40 minutes
Day 4	Walk 20–30 minutes	Jog 6.4km (4 miles)	Cycle 40 minutes	Swim 40 minutes	Jog 9.7km (6 miles)
Day 5	Rest day	Rest day	Jog 8km (5 miles)	Jog 6.4km (4 miles)	Rest day
Day 6	Resistance training, 20 minutes	Jog 6.4km (4 miles)	Cycle 40 minutes	Rest day	Jog 9.7km (6 miles)
Day 7	Rest day	Jog 6.4km (4 miles)	Jog 4.8km (3 miles)	Jog 9.7km (6 miles)	Jog 6.4km (4 miles)
Total distance run:	0	19.3km (12 miles)	25.7km (16 miles)	32.2km (20 miles)	45km (28 miles)

Note: All training should be done at an easy, conversational pace. Do not resume any hard, anaerobic training until after this build-up period.

5KM RACING PROGRAMME

Events at this distance are plentiful and can be perfect for the beginner and advanced runner alike. For someone new to racing, this event offers a manageable and non-threatening introductory distance, and for advanced racers, it can be an excellent opportunity for speed training. This training programme, however, is geared towards the first-time racer who should be training at conversational pace throughout. The programme on the right is meant to be used as a guideline, and not an exact formula for your workouts.

Weeks 1–4 If you've never run 1.6km (1 mile) before, your body will be adjusting to running this additional distance during the first two weeks. This will probably last only 14 days, but your body may still be adjusting up until week four. Set your goals carefully, and do not overreach yourself.

Weeks 5–8 You should be feeling comfortable with the distances you've been running in the first four weeks, and now that your body has adjusted, your running is ready for improvement. Listen to your body and increase your distance slowly.

Weeks 9–12 By week ten, you should be approaching your peak fitness for distances of about 5km (3.1 miles). During week ten, increase your pace and/or distance very slightly. For the final two weeks, slightly taper your training by at least 30 per cent to avoid burnout and injury.

Rest days
Run days

	Day 1	Day 2
WEEK 1	Jog 1.6km (1 mile)	Rest day
WEEK 2	Day 8 Jog 1.6km (1 mile)	Day 9 Rest day
WEEK 3	Day 15 Rest day	Day 16 Jog 2.4km (1.5 miles)
WEEK 4	Day 22 Rest day	Day 23 Jog 2.4km (1.5 miles)
WEEK 5	Day 29 Jog 3.2km (2 miles)	Day 30 Rest day
WEEK 6	Day 36 Rest day	Day 37 Jog 3.2km (2 miles)
WEEK 7	Day 43 Rest day	Day 44 Jog 4km (2.5 miles)
WEEK 8	Day 50 Jog 4km (2.5 miles)	Day 51 Rest day
WEEK 9	Day 57 Rest day	Day 58 Jog 4.8km (3 miles)
WEEK 10	Day 64 Jog 4.8km (3 miles)	Day 65 Rest day
WEEK 11	Day 71 Rest day	Day 72 Jog 4km (2.5 miles)
WEEK 12	Day 78 Jog 3.2km (2 miles)	Day 79 Rest day

Day 3	Day 4	Day 5	Day 6	Day 7	Total
Jog 1.6km (1 mile)	Rest day	Jog 1.6km (1 mile)	Rest day	Rest day	4.8km (3 miles)
Day 10 Jog 1.6km (1 mile)	**Day 11** Rest day	**Day 12** Jog 1.6km (1 mile)	**Day 13** Rest day	**Day 14** Jog 1.6km (1 mile)	**Total** 6.4km (4 miles)
Day 17 Rest day	**Day 18** Jog 2.4km (1.5 miles)	**Day 19** Rest day	**Day 20** Jog 2.4km (1.5 miles)	**Day 21** Jog 2.4km (1.5 miles)	**Total** 9.7km (6 miles)
Day 24 Rest day	**Day 25** Jog 2.4km (1.5 miles)	**Day 26** Jog 2.4km (1.5 miles)	**Day 27** Rest day	**Day 28** Jog 2.4km (1.5 miles)	**Total** 9.7km (6 miles)
Day 31 Jog 3.2km (2 miles)	**Day 32** Rest day	**Day 33** Jog 3.2km (2 miles)	**Day 34** Rest day	**Day 35** Jog 3.2km (2 miles)	**Total** 12.9km (8 miles)
Day 38 Rest day	**Day 39** Jog 3.2km (2 miles)	**Day 40** Rest day	**Day 41** Jog 3.2km (2 miles)	**Day 42** Jog 3.2km (2 miles)	**Total** 12.9km (8 miles)
Day 45 Rest day	**Day 46** Jog 4km (2.5 miles)	**Day 47** Rest day	**Day 48** Jog 4km (2.5 miles)	**Day 49** Jog 4km (2.5 miles)	**Total** 16km (10 miles)
Day 52 Jog 4km (2.5 miles)	**Day 53** Rest day	**Day 54** Jog 4km (2.5 miles)	**Day 55** Jog 4km (2.5 miles)	**Day 56** Rest day	**Total** 16km (10 miles)
Day 59 Rest day	**Day 60** Jog 4.8km (3 miles)	**Day 61** Jog 4.8km (3 miles)	**Day 62** Rest day	**Day 63** Jog 4.8km (3 miles)	**Total** 19.3km (12 miles)
Day 66 Jog 5.6km (3.5 miles)	**Day 67** Rest day	**Day 68** Jog 4.8km (3 miles)	**Day 69** Jog 5.6km (3.5 miles)	**Day 70** Rest day	**Total** 20.9km (13 miles)
Day 73 Rest day	**Day 74** Jog 4km (2.5 miles)	**Day 75** Rest day	**Day 76** Jog 4km (2.5 miles)	**Day 77** Rest day	**Total** 12km (7.5 miles)
Day 80 Jog 3.2km (2 miles)	**Day 81** Rest day	**Day 82** Jog 3.2km (2 miles)	**Day 83** Rest day	**Day 84** Rest day	**Total** 9.7km (6 miles)

10KM RACING PROGRAMME

Events at this distance are great for intermediate runners looking for a new challenge after running a few 5km (3.1-mile) races. As with 5km (3.1-mile) races, advanced racers may wish to run 10km (6.2-mile) races as part of their speed training. Those training for a half-marathon, but new to racing, should also consider running a 10km (6.2-mile) race first to familiarize themselves with how a race feels. This basic training programme is aimed at the intermediate racer, and all workouts are meant to be done at conversational pace. You may incorporate one interval training workout (see pp112–15) per week if you wish. The programme on the right is meant to be used as a guideline, and not an exact formula for your workouts.

Weeks 1–4 If you've never run more than 5km (3.1 miles) before, your body will be adjusting to running this additional distance during the first two weeks. This will probably last only 14 days, but your body may still be adjusting up until week four. Set your goals carefully, and do not overreach yourself.

Weeks 5–8 You should be feeling comfortable with the distances you've been running in the first four weeks, and now that your body has adjusted, your running is ready for improvement. Listen to your body and increase your distance slowly, or add one weekly interval training session.

Weeks 9–12 By week ten you should be approaching your peak fitness for distances of about 10km (6.2 miles). During week ten, increase your pace and/or distance very slightly. For the final two weeks, taper your training by at least 30 per cent to avoid burnout and injury.

| | Rest days |
| | Run days |

	Day 1	Day 2
WEEK 1	Jog 4.8km (3 miles)	Rest day

	Day 8	Day 9
WEEK 2	Jog 5.6km (3.5 miles)	Rest day

	Day 15	Day 16
WEEK 3	Jog 5.6km (3.5 miles)	Jog 5.6km (3.5 miles)

	Day 22	Day 23
WEEK 4	Rest day	Jog 6.4km (4 miles)

	Day 29	Day 30
WEEK 5	Jog 6.4km (4 miles)	Rest day

	Day 36	Day 37
WEEK 6	Rest day	Jog 7.2km (4.5 miles)

	Day 43	Day 44
WEEK 7	Rest day	Jog 8km (5 miles)

	Day 50	Day 51
WEEK 8	Jog 8.6km (5.5 miles)	Rest day

	Day 57	Day 58
WEEK 9	Rest day	Jog 9.7km (6 miles)

	Day 64	Day 65
WEEK 10	Jog 4.8km (3 miles)	Rest day

	Day 71	Day 72
WEEK 11	Rest day	Jog 6.4km (4 miles)

	Day 78	Day 79
WEEK 12	Jog 5.6km (3.5 miles)	Rest day

Day 3	Day 4	Day 5	Day 6	Day 7	Total
Jog 4.8km (3 miles)	Rest day	Jog 4.8km (3 miles)	Rest day	Rest day	14.4km (9 miles)
Day 10	**Day 11**	**Day 12**	**Day 13**	**Day 14**	**Total**
Jog 5.6km (3.5 miles)	Rest day	Jog 5.6km (3.5 miles)	Rest day	Jog 5.6km (3.5 miles)	22.5km (14 miles)
Day 17	**Day 18**	**Day 19**	**Day 20**	**Day 21**	**Total**
Rest day	Jog 4.8km (3 miles)	Rest day	Jog 5.6km (3.5 miles)	Jog 2.4km (1.5 miles)	28.2km (17.5 miles)
Day 24	**Day 25**	**Day 26**	**Day 27**	**Day 28**	**Total**
Rest day	Jog 6.4km (4 miles)	Jog 6.4km (4 miles)	Rest day	Jog 6.4km (4 miles)	25.8km (16 miles)
Day 31	**Day 32**	**Day 33**	**Day 34**	**Day 35**	**Total**
Jog 5.6km (3.5 miles)	Rest day	Jog 6.4km (4 miles)	Rest day	Jog 7.2km (4.5 miles)	25.8km (16 miles)
Day 38	**Day 39**	**Day 40**	**Day 41**	**Day 42**	**Total**
Rest day	Jog 8km (5 miles)	Rest day	Jog 8km (5 miles)	Jog 8km (5 miles)	31.2km (19.5 miles)
Day 45	**Day 46**	**Day 47**	**Day 48**	**Day 49**	**Total**
Rest day	Jog 7.2km (4.5 miles)	Rest day	Jog 8km (5 miles)	Jog 8km (5 miles)	31.2km (19.5 miles)
Day 52	**Day 53**	**Day 54**	**Day 55**	**Day 56**	**Total**
Jog 8.6km (5.5 miles)	Rest day	Jog 8.6km (5.5 miles)	Jog 8.6km (5.5 miles)	Rest day	35.4km (22 miles)
Day 59	**Day 60**	**Day 61**	**Day 62**	**Day 63**	**Total**
Rest day	Jog 9.7km (6 miles)	Jog 8.6km (5.5 miles)	Rest day	Jog 10.5km (6.5 miles)	35.4km (22 miles)
Day 66	**Day 67**	**Day 68**	**Day 69**	**Day 70**	**Total**
Jog 9.7km (6 miles)	Rest day	Jog 10.5km (6.5 miles)	Jog 8.6km (5.5 miles)	Rest day	39.4km (24.5 miles)
Day 73	**Day 74**	**Day 75**	**Day 76**	**Day 77**	**Total**
Jog 6.4km (4 miles)	Jog 6.4km (4 miles)	Rest day	Jog 6.4km (4 miles)	Rest day	25.8km (16 miles)
Day 80	**Day 81**	**Day 82**	**Day 83**	**Day 84**	**Total**
Jog 6.4km (4 miles)	Rest day	Jog 4.8km (3 miles)	Jog 6.4km (4 miles)	Rest day	23.3km (14.5 miles)

HALF-MARATHON PROGRAMME

The half-marathon (21km/13.1 miles) is a great middle-distance race that offers a wonderful sense of achievement for all intermediate and advanced runners. Before training for this event, you should have already run a few 10km (6.2-mile) races to familiarize yourself with racing. Half-marathons are particularly good training for runners planning on doing a future marathon. This basic training programme is aimed at the intermediate racer, and all workouts are meant to be done at conversational pace. You may incorporate one interval training workout per week, if you wish (see pp112–15). The programme on the right is meant to be used as a guideline, and not an exact formula for your workouts.

Weeks 1–4 If you've never run more than 10km (6.2 miles) before, your body will be adjusting to running this additional distance during the first two weeks. This will probably last only 14 days, but your body may still be adjusting up until week four. Set your goals carefully, and do not overreach yourself.

Weeks 5–8 You should be feeling comfortable with the distances you've been running in the first four weeks, and now that your body has adjusted, your running is ready for improvement. Listen to your body and increase your distance slowly. From now on, you may replace one weekly workout (excluding your long run, marked by asterisks on the right) with an interval training session (see pp112–17).

Weeks 9–12 By week ten you should be approaching your peak fitness for distances of about 21km (13.1 miles). During week ten, increase your pace and/or distance very slightly. For the final two weeks, slightly taper your training by at least 30 per cent to avoid burnout and injury.

| | Rest days |
| | Run days |

	Day 1	Day 2
WEEK 1	Jog 9.7km (6 miles)	Rest day

	Day 8	Day 9
WEEK 2	Jog 10.5km (6.5 miles)	Rest day

	Day 15	Day 16
WEEK 3	Rest day	Jog 8km (5 mile)

	Day 22	Day 23
WEEK 4	Rest day	Jog 10.5km (6.5 miles)

	Day 29	Day 30
WEEK 5	Jog 9.7km (6 miles)	Rest day

	Day 36	Day 37
WEEK 6	Rest day	Jog 10.5km (6.5 miles)

	Day 43	Day 44
WEEK 7	Rest day	Jog 11.3km (7 miles)

	Day 50	Day 51
WEEK 8	Jog 11.3km (7 miles)	Rest day

	Day 57	Day 58
WEEK 9	Rest day	Jog 11.3km (7 miles)

	Day 64	Day 65
WEEK 10	Jog 11.3km (7 miles)*	Jog 10.5km (6.5 miles)

	Day 71	Day 72
WEEK 11	Jog 10.5km (6.5 miles)	Jog 4km (2.5 miles)

	Day 78	Day 79
WEEK 12	Jog 3.2km (2 miles)	Rest day

Day 3	Day 4	Day 5	Day 6	Day 7	Total
Jog 9.7km (6 miles)	Rest day	Jog 6.4km (4 miles)	Rest day	Jog 9.7km (6 miles)	35.4km (22 miles)

Day 10	Day 11	Day 12	Day 13	Day 14	Total
Jog 10.5km (6.5 miles)	Rest day	Jog 6.4km (4 miles)	Rest day	Jog 11.3km (7 miles)*	38.6km (24 miles)

Day 17	Day 18	Day 19	Day 20	Day 21	Total
Rest day	Jog 10.5km (6.5 miles)	Rest day	Jog 9.7km (6 miles)	Jog 12.9km (8 miles)*	41km (25.5 miles)

Day 24	Day 25	Day 26	Day 27	Day 28	Total
Rest day	Jog 10.5km (6.5 miles)	Jog 8km (5 mile)	Rest day	Jog 14.5km (9 miles)*	43.5km (27 miles)

Day 31	Day 32	Day 33	Day 34	Day 35	Total
Jog 12.9km (8 miles)	Rest day	Jog 10.5km (6.5 miles)	Rest day	Jog 16.1km (10 miles)*	49.1km (30.5 miles)

Day 38	Day 39	Day 40	Day 41	Day 42	Total
Rest day	Jog 12.9km (8 miles)	Rest day	Jog 10.5km (6.5 miles)	Jog 16.9km (10.5 miles)*	50.7km (31.5 miles)

Day 45	Day 46	Day 47	Day 48	Day 49	Total
Rest day	Jog 11.3km (7 miles)	Rest day	Jog 12.9km (8 miles)	Jog 17.8km (11 miles)*	53.1km (33 miles)

Day 52	Day 53	Day 54	Day 55	Day 56	Total
Jog 11.3km (7 miles)	Rest day	Jog 4km (2.5 miles)	Rest day	Jog 18.5km (11.5 miles)*	55.5km (34.5 miles)

Day 59	Day 60	Day 61	Day 62	Day 63	Total
Rest day	Jog 14.5km (9 miles)	Jog 11.3km (7 miles)	Rest day	Jog 19.3km (12 miles)*	56.3km (35 miles)

Day 66	Day 67	Day 68	Day 69	Day 70	Total
Jog 11.3km (7 miles)	Rest day	Jog 10.5km (6.5 miles)	Rest day	Jog 21.7km (13.5 miles)*	65.2km (40.5 miles)

Day 73	Day 74	Day 75	Day 76	Day 77	Total
Jog 10.5km (6.5 miles)	Rest day	Jog 6.4km (4 miles)	Rest day	Jog 11.3km (7 miles)	38.6km (24 miles)

Day 80	Day 81	Day 82	Day 83	Day 84	Total
Jog 9.7km (6 miles)	Rest day	Jog 6.4km (4 miles)	Rest day	Jog 9.7km (6 miles)	35.4km (22 miles)

MARATHON PROGRAMME

The marathon (42.1km/26.2 miles) is the holy grail among road races for intermediate and advanced runners. The great thing about it is that, if trained properly, just about anyone can run a marathon. This programme builds on the half-marathon training programme (see pp152–53). You should have run at least one half-marathon (or preferably two or three) before training for a marathon – it will give you a good idea of how your body will respond to long-distance racing. You should also choose your race wisely, picking a course that is similar in landscape and climate to where you've been training. So, if you've been training in a flat, cool city, pick a race with a flat course in a cool climate.

This basic training programme is aimed at the intermediate racer, and all workouts are meant to be done at conversational pace. You may replace one shorter run per week with an interval training workout if you wish (see pp112–15). The programme on the right is meant to be used as a guideline, and not an exact formula for your workouts.

Weeks 1–4 If you've never run more than 10km (6.2 miles) before, your body will be adjusting to running this additional distance during the first two weeks. This will probably last only 14 days, but your body may still be adjusting up until week four. Set your goals carefully, and do not overreach yourself.

Weeks 5–8 You should be feeling comfortable with the distances you've been running in the first four weeks, and now that your body has adjusted, your running is ready for improvement. Listen to your body and increase your distance slowly. From now on, you may replace one weekly workout (excluding your long run, marked by asterisks on the right) with an interval training session.

Weeks 9–12 By week nine you should be approaching your peak fitness for distances of about 30.6–32.2km (19–20 miles). During week ten, you may wish to increase your pace and/or distance very slightly. There is no need to exceed 35.4km (22 miles) in your runs – running distances greater than this in training can be harmful to your body. For the final two weeks, taper your training by at least 30 per cent to avoid burnout and injury (for more details, see pp132–33).

Rest days
Run days

WEEK 1	Day 1	Day 2
	Jog 9.7km (6 miles)	Rest day

WEEK 2	Day 8	Day 9
	Jog 9.7km (6 miles)	Rest day

WEEK 3	Day 15	Day 16
	Rest day	Jog 9.7km (6 miles)

WEEK 4	Day 22	Day 23
	Rest day	Jog 9.7km (6 miles)

WEEK 5	Day 29	Day 30
	Jog 11.3km (7 miles)	Rest day

WEEK 6	Day 36	Day 37
	Rest day	Jog 11.3km (7 miles)

WEEK 7	Day 43	Day 44
	Rest day	Jog 11.3km (7 miles)

WEEK 8	Day 50	Day 51
	Jog 11.3km (7 miles)	Rest day

WEEK 9	Day 57	Day 58
	Rest day	Jog 9.7km (6 miles)

WEEK 10	Day 64	Day 65
	Jog 11.3km (7 miles)	Rest day

WEEK 11	Day 71	Day 72
	Jog 9.7km (6 miles)	Rest day

WEEK 12	Day 78	Day 79
	Jog 9.7km (6 miles)	Jog 9.7km (6 miles)

Day 3	Day 4	Day 5	Day 6	Day 7	Total
Jog 9.7km (6 miles)	Rest day	Jog 6.4km (4 miles)	Rest day	Jog 16.1km (10 miles)*	41.9km (26 miles)

Day 10	Day 11	Day 12	Day 13	Day 14	Total
Jog 11.3km (7 miles)	Rest day	Jog 8km (5 miles)	Rest day	Jog 19.3km (12 miles)*	48.3km (30 miles)

Day 17	Day 18	Day 19	Day 20	Day 21	Total
Rest day	Jog 11.3km (7 miles)	Rest day	Jog 9.7km (6 miles)	Jog 20.9km (13 miles)*	51.6km (32 miles)

Day 24	Day 25	Day 26	Day 27	Day 28	Total
Rest day	Jog 12.9km (8 miles)	Jog 9.7km (6 miles)	Rest day	Jog 19.3km (12 miles)*	51.6km (32 miles)

Day 31	Day 32	Day 33	Day 34	Day 35	Total
Jog 14.5km (9 miles)	Rest day	Jog 9.7km (6 miles)	Rest day	Jog 24.1km (15 miles)*	59.6km (37 miles)

Day 38	Day 39	Day 40	Day 41	Day 42	Total
Rest day	Jog 14.5km (9 miles)	Rest day	Jog 9.7km (6 miles)	Jog 25.7km (16 miles)*	61.2km (38 miles)

Day 45	Day 46	Day 47	Day 48	Day 49	Total
Rest day	Jog 11.3km (7 miles)	Rest day	Jog 12.9km (8 miles)	Jog 27.4km (17 miles)*	62.9km (39 miles)

Day 52	Day 53	Day 54	Day 55	Day 56	Total
Jog 11.3km (7 miles)	Rest day	Jog 12.9km (8 miles)	Rest day	Jog 29km (18 miles)*	64.4km (40 miles)

Day 59	Day 60	Day 61	Day 62	Day 63	Total
Rest day	Jog 14.5km (9 miles)	Jog 9.7km (6 miles)	Rest day	Jog 30.6km (19 miles)*	64.4km (40 miles)

Day 66	Day 67	Day 68	Day 69	Day 70	Total
Jog 9.7km (6 miles)	Rest day	Jog 12.9km (8 miles)	Rest day	Jog 32.2km (20 miles)*	66km (41 miles)

Day 73	Day 74	Day 75	Day 76	Day 77	Total
Jog 9.7km (6 miles)	Jog 9.7km (6 miles)	Rest day	Jog 9.7km (6 miles)	Jog 6.4km (4 miles)	45km (28 miles)

Day 80	Day 81	Day 82	Day 83	Day 84	Total
Jog 9.7km (6 miles)	Jog 9.7km (6 miles)	Rest day	Jog 6.4km (4 miles)	Rest day	45km (28 miles)

INDEX

ACKNOWLEDGMENTS

Author's acknowledgments

Giving acknowledgments for me means expressing profound thanks to a few of the many wonderful people who mentored and encouraged me as I pursued my well guarded Olympic goals. I now realize how blessed I have been. First, to my running and lifetime teammates at Yale University, who simply taught me how to think while running. Dr Ken Davis, my Yale roommate, who showed me how to truly focus. Jimmy Carnes in Florida and Bill Bowerman at the Munich Olympics – men who unwittingly made it so much easier for me to focus on my training. In my post-Olympic years George Hirsch was there to emulate as I figured out how to earn a living while still staying connected to the sport I love. Over the years, Joe French, Bob Stone, and Steve Bosley, along with other close friends in my adopted home of Boulder, Colorado, have helped provide the perfect living and training venue for me. To my fiancée Michelle, as we move forward in life together. On the editorial side, to Gillian Roberts and Mary-Clare Jerram for trusting that I could write this book in what I hope is a truly understandable manner. Thanks also to Miranda Harvey and Russell Sadur for the book's beautiful layout and photography, and to Shannon Beatty for helping me direct my thoughts when they chose to wander.

Publisher's acknowledgments

Dorling Kindersley would like to thank photographer Russell Sadur and his assistant Nina Duncan; models Amy Colby, Simon Harley, Leslie Herod, Gina Mangum, Sheree Matheson, and Thea Thompson; Catherine Corona, for the models' hair and makeup; the Flatiron Athletic Club; Rosamund Cox for editorial assistance; Laura Clark for consultancy services; and Christopher Beatty and Eric Dubrow, for their helpful advice.

Thanks also to Frank Shorter Sports for supplying running clothes, New Balance for running shoes, and Julian Wolk at ChampionChipUK for lending us a ChampionChip®.

Picture credits

Asics: p.23; Alamy/Image100: p.86; Alamy/Popperfoto: p.88; Getty Images: Julian Finney: p.91 All other images © DK Images

ABOUT THE AUTHOR

Frank Shorter achieved the highest accolade in running by winning the gold medal in the Olympic marathon in Munich, Germany in 1972. He then went on to win the silver medal in the following 1976 Olympic Games held in Montreal, Canada.

Among his many athletic achievements, Frank is a five-time United States national 10,000-metre champion and a four-time national cross-country champion. Having also won the Fukuoka International Marathon in Japan four years in a row, Frank is now a member of the United States Olympic Hall of Fame.

Frank is a 1969 graduate of Yale University with a degree in Psychology, having also studied in its Premedical Programme. He went on to receive a law degree from the University of Florida, and passed the Colorado Bar Exam in 1975. In 1977, he set up his company Frank Shorter Sports, which develops running gear for the serious athlete.

Frank is the founding chairman of the US Anti-Doping Agency, working in support of anti-doping initiatives to free Olympic sports from legal, performance-enhancing drugs. A Special Contributor for the American edition of Runner's World magazine, he is also a commentator for NBC-TV Sports in the US. He lives in Boulder, Colorado.

Every effort has been made to ensure that the information in this book is accurate. However, neither the publisher, nor the author, nor anyone else involved in the preparation of this book are engaged in rendering professional advice or services to the individual reader. Always consult your doctor before starting a fitness and/or nutrition programme if you have any health concerns.

SECOND EDITION
Editor Amy Slack
Designer Philippa Nash
Jacket designer Steven Marsden
Pre-production producer Tony Phipps
Producer Stephanie McConnell
Managing editor Stephanie Farrow
Managing art editor Christine Keilty

FIRST EDITION
Project editor Shannon Beatty
Art editor Miranda Harvey
Managing editor Stephanie Farrow
Publishing manager Gillian Roberts
Art director Carole Ash
Publishing director Mary-Clare Jerram
DTP designer Sonia Charbonnier
Production controller Sarah Dodd
Photographer Russell Sadur

This edition published in 2018
First published in Great Britain in 2005 by
Dorling Kindersley Limited
80 Strand, London, WC2R 0RL

Copyright © 2005, 2018 Dorling Kindersley Limited
A Penguin Random House Company
10 9 8 7 6 5 4 3 2 1
001–305956–Apr/2018
Text copyright © 2005 Frank Shorter

A CIP catalogue record for this book
is available from the British Library.
ISBN: 978-0-2413-0208-8

Printed and bound in China

A WORLD OF IDEAS:
SEE ALL THERE IS TO KNOW

www.dk.com